Divine Alignment

"Let the Magick Begin"

Copyright © 2025 iC7Zi.
All rights reserved.
Published by iC7Zi

Table of Contents

Preface	4
Section I — Divine Alignment	
Introduction	19
The Foundations of Hermetic Philosophy	25
The Tripartite Model of Humans	43
Understanding the Spirit	54
The Alchemy of Existence	61
The Principle of Mentalism	67
Reincarnation in Hermetic Philosophy	80
Summary	89
Section II — The Demiurge and the Hidden God	
Introduction	97
Defining Demiurge	100
Historical Overview	103
Philosophical Context	108
Symbols of the Demiurge	112
Demiurge in Religious Texts	120
The Great Reveal	127
The Human Journey	139

Section III — Alchemical Training	
Introduction	144
Emerging from the Shadows	148
The Embrace of the Self	154
Unshakable Pillars	160
Walking Through Fire	167
Mastering the Inner Realm	174
The Fortress Within	180
The River of Feelings	186
A World of Connections	192
Golden Transitions	198
Beyond the Stars	204
In Mastery of the Self	212

Preface

Hello there, fellow traveler! You've just opened the door to a rather unique journey, a kind of compass for wandering the intricate maze of your soul. Consider this your personal invite to an exciting exploration of your inner universe. And just so you know, this is only the introduction—a playful opener to the deeper and richer thoughts we'll soon explore together.

So, here you are, and let me assure you, this exact spot, this very moment, is precisely where you're meant to be. Yes, right here, reading these words—no need for GPS coordinates or a time machine. As the wise old saying goes, "Wherever you go, there you are," and what better place to start than smack-dab in the middle of now and right here?

Throughout the ages, humanity has been captivated by the mysteries of existence. What lies beyond the material world? What forces shape our reality? And, most profoundly, how can we align ourselves with these forces to uncover deeper meaning and purpose? Divine Alignment: Let the Magick Begin invites you to embark on a journey into these timeless questions through the lens of ancient wisdom, spiritual insights, and transformative practices.

At the heart of this journey lies a central truth: we are co-creators of our reality. From the ancient temples of Delphi, where seekers were exhorted to "know thyself," to the Hermetic principle that "The All is Mind; the Universe is Mental," great traditions have pointed to the profound connection between the inner and outer worlds. This book is an exploration of that connection—a call to awaken your inner magick and align with the divine essence within and around you.

This book is all about embracing the full spectrum of your existence with acceptance, grace, and a hefty dollop of mindfulness. It's about discovering that every moment, even this one as you ponder over these words, holds infinite potential for growth and transformation. We're not just spinning in circles here; we're spiraling upwards, or downwards, or whichever way your soul needs to soar.

Life, my friend, is quite the spectacle, a pendulum swinging wildly between highs and lows. Imagine we're actors in an elaborate play set on a spinning rock, orbiting a giant fireball. Wild, isn't it? You might wonder why bother with all the effort. Well, why not? Isn't there a spark within you that yearns to glow brighter, to taste improvement?

> Oh, the inner worlds we tread,
> Spun of dreams and woven thread;
> Beneath the surface calm, a sea,
> Where shadows dance and spirits free.

Now, don't let the breezy tone fool you; we'll get serious soon enough. There will be moments as dense as a double chocolate cake and perhaps as bitter as the darkest coffee you've dared to sip. But remember, the journey of a thousand miles begins with a single step—or in this case, a flip of the page.

So, with a wink and a nudge, let's gear up. Strap on your metaphorical boots, pack your sense of humor, and maybe bring a snack or two for the road (journeys through the psyche can be surprisingly munchy work). Let's set forth with the wind of curiosity at our backs, and a map etched not in ink, but in dreams and possibilities.

As you navigate through these pages, keep in mind that the reality of where you are now is the perfect place to start. With a chuckle and a cheer, we embark not just to explore but to revel in the journey. And who knows? By the end of this book, you might just find that the person walking out of this labyrinth isn't quite the person who walked in.

Ready? Let's turn the page and begin, and remember, as Mark Twain might have chuckled, "The secret of getting ahead is getting started." And start we shall, right at this wonderfully right place and this most opportune time.

As Joseph Campbell Said,

> We have not even to risk the adventure alone for the heroes of all time have gone before us. The labyrinth is thoroughly known...

we have only to follow the thread of the hero path. And where we had thought to find an abomination we shall find a God. And where we had thought to slay another we shall slay ourselves. Where we had thought to travel outwards we shall come to the center of our own existence. And where we had thought to be alone we shall be with all the world.

Embracing the Abyss

Let me paint you a picture of a landscape hidden within us all, a place where fear, despair, and the scattered fragments of dreams yet to mend come together in a haunting dance. Picture this as the abyss, the so-called Dark Night of the Soul. It's not just a crisis; it's a mysterious call to transformation that's louder than any siren's song. This isn't about packing bags for a journey around the world, but rather, it's a voyage into the cavernous depths of our very essence.

Imagine standing at the edge of this abyss. It strips everything away, leaving you stark and bare, facing the rawness of who you are without any frills. It's a place where all your masks fall away, and what's left is just the core of your being, trembling and unadorned.

Many stumble into this profound depth when life throws its curveballs—grief, failure, betrayal, or that echoing emptiness that lurks beneath even the most glittering successes. But what if we chose to dive in? What if we saw this not as a fall but as a deliberate leap toward something new, a rebirth waiting in the shadowy depths?

Walt Whitman once said, "Not I, nor anyone else can travel that road for you. You must travel it by yourself." And it's true, especially here, in the abyss. It demands a confrontation with every demon of doubt, fear, and unworthiness. But here's the secret: this confrontation is actually the hidden path to freedom.

Navigating this shadowy realm requires some unique tools, not the physical kind but those crafted from the spirit and the mind. Awareness is the first tool—sharp, unflinching. It's about watching your every thought and emotion, recognizing the patterns that have shackled you. Through awareness, we start to see the abyss not as a punishment but as a rich, albeit stern, teacher.

Then comes acceptance. Fighting the abyss only feeds it, makes it larger, more daunting. Acceptance is the gentle art of meeting reality head-on, without flinching or turning away, recognizing things just as they are. It's about finding peace with the present, which paradoxically, is the first step to transforming it.

And don't forget intuition—that soft, steady voice within that knows the way even when all maps fail. In the abyss, where familiar landmarks vanish, this voice is your unwavering guide. It calls for a quiet mind and a courageous heart, a trust in the wisdom that bubbles up when you least expect it.

For those who dare to endure, the abyss reveals itself not as an endless void but as a womb brimming with potential. The ego dissolves, and with it, the shadows lose their terror and become guardians of profound truths. Here lies the strength born of vulnerability, the wisdom that springs from hardship, and the pure, exhilarating joy of being utterly, authentically yourself.

"The only journey is the one within," Rilke reminds us. The abyss, then, is not a curse but a hidden blessing, a mysterious invitation to the grandest adventure—the exploration of the deepest, most intricate chambers of the human heart.

Life, my friend, is quite the spectacle, a pendulum swinging wildly between highs and lows. Imagine we're actors in an elaborate play set on a spinning rock, orbiting a giant fireball. Wild, isn't it? You might wonder why bother with all the effort. Well, why not? Isn't there a spark within you that yearns to glow brighter, to taste improvement?

And sure, someone might toss out, "What's the point? We're all headed towards the same grand finale: death." But I'd say, why not live with gusto, squeeze every drop of joy from your days before the curtain falls? Then comes the retort, "But highs lead to lows, and I'm weary of this endless cycle." Yes, the ride is dizzying, and it's enough to make anyone dizzy.

Here's a slice of advice—be the observer. Don't get too attached to the highs and don't dread the lows. Stop the endless comparisons, the gratitude that whispers of superiority. Just be. It is what it is. Our script on this celestial stage is somewhat pre-written; our freewill isn't as free as we'd like to think. So, when the credits roll, or the dark night of the soul creeps in, remember, you didn't audition for this role in life's play, so face the final act bravely.

At the end of the day, we're all in this game, some are aware of the rules, and some are just tagging along. And hey, let me drop a little secret—miracles do happen, but they like a bit of elbow grease, a bit of intention. Keep pushing, not because you owe it to the world, but for the sheer, stubborn sake of being. And if you're tired, rest. You don't owe anyone anything, and nobody owes you.

So here we are, twirling through the cosmos, each of us juggling our bits of chaos and stars. Keep dancing through it all, for yourself, for the whole wild, inexplicable shebang. And if you feel like sitting one out, that's perfectly fine too.

As you traverse your own abyss, remember, you're in good company. Many have walked this path before, their voices whispering courage and companionship in the silent stretches of your journey. So, armed with awareness, acceptance, and intuition, let's step boldly forward. After all, this path through the shadows is the very road to discovering our truest selves.

The Alchemy of Chaos

Imagine standing at the edge of a storm, where the wind howls like a chorus of wild spirits and chaos seems to rule unchallenged. This is where transformation beckons—the kind that shapes souls and sculpts destinies. It's not a stroll through a sunny park; this journey demands a lion-hearted kind of bravery, resilience, and an unwavering trust in the glow of your inner spark.

As we navigate this tempest within, we dive into an alchemical mystery, turning our deepest fears and doubts into shining gold of wisdom and enlightenment. Inside this whirlwind of emotions and thoughts, it may seem like we're being torn apart, but as Carl Jung masterfully pointed out, "In all chaos there is a cosmos, in all disorder a secret order."

Within the swirling mayhem of our inner landscapes lies the fertile soil from which our true selves can emerge, vibrant and full of life. Embracing this turmoil isn't about being swallowed by it, but rather mastering the art of sailing its wild currents with elegance and insight.

Delving into our shadows isn't for the faint-hearted. It's about facing and integrating the aspects we've often turned away from or buried. Jung again whispers wisdom from the depths, "One does not become enlightened by imagining figures of light, but by making the darkness conscious." This shadow work is crucial for authenticity and wholeness, lighting up the entire spectrum of who we are.

This voyage through inner storms is intensely personal, uncharted by others' maps. While the wisdom of spiritual mentors and ancient traditions can guide us, our path must be forged from our own experiences, our own inner knowing—this is gnosis. It's a profound, direct knowledge that springs from deep within, pointing us toward our truest purpose.

To navigate these waters, we anchor ourselves with practices like meditation, journaling, and creative expression. These tools help us tune into our inner voice, decipher the subtle signals amidst the uproar, revealing the lessons hidden in chaos.

In the deepest darkness of our journey, hope and faith light the way—not as naive optimism, but as profound trust in the transformative process. Desmond Tutu beautifully captures this spirit, "Hope is being able to see that there is light despite all of the darkness." This kind of hope, along with a deep faith in our own resilience and the transformative power of both love and struggle, propels us forward.

Through the alchemy of our inner chaos, we are reborn, realigned with our deepest truths and loftiest dreams. This rebirth isn't a regression to innocence but a conscious, harmonious reintegration of our entire being.

Emerging from the storm, we aren't the same people who entered. We're reshaped, enlightened by our trials, balancing light and dark, order and chaos, in a dance as old as time. This journey doesn't just enlighten us; it connects us more deeply with the world, revealing that the patterns of chaos and order, light and darkness, are woven into the fabric of everything that exists.

We're here, alive and kicking on this big blue ball, and the wildest part? We're aware of it. Think about that for a second—we're part of the cosmic lineup, and we know it. It's up to each of us to sketch out what life means on our own personal canvases. Sure, we get hints along the way—those quirky little things called intuitions and synchronicities that whisper clues about our purpose. And while there are some universal gigs, like spreading a little compassion around, much of this gig is a solo act.

The real magic happens inside us. Once we sort out the inner chaos, the outer world starts to fall into place. It's kind of like tuning into a new wavelength—quantum field style. It sounds like the latest buzz, but really, it's an ancient tune played on new instruments. And here's the kicker: the tune is simple, but learning to play it? That's the tough part. It's not about overnight enlightenment or quick fixes; it's a long game full of trial and error.

The best trick up your sleeve? Pull up a chair, sit down, and just breathe. Watch your breath like you're watching the slowest Netflix series ever. Ever seen a sloth? Here's a fun challenge: be a sloth for a day. Slow down, way down. Feel every moment, experience it, soak it in, and let it simmer. See what insights bubble up when you dial down the pace and really tune in.

So, let's march into the storm with hearts full of hope, faith in our pockets, and eyes open to the potential within us to turn our darkest nights into our brightest dawns, moving with the deliberate grace of a sloth, embracing each moment fully as it comes.

The Quest for Personal Myth

Picture yourself on a mysterious night, the kind where shadows stretch long and deep, cast by our own doubts and fears. In this enigmatic darkness, there's a profound truth waiting quietly, ready to be uncovered. Joseph Campbell might say that this shadowy ordeal is not a blockade but a passage, a vital part of our hero's journey toward self-discovery and crafting our personal myth. He once wisely noted, "The cave you fear to enter holds the treasure you seek."

In this shadowy confrontation, we're not just facing our demons; we're on the brink of discovering our unique destiny, a dream distinct from the hand-me-down aspirations shaped by tradition or others' expectations.

This journey through the dark night is unending, a perpetual cycle of despair and enlightenment that molds the very contours of our soul. Here, we stumble upon gnosis—a deep, intuitive understanding that leaps beyond mere intellectual knowledge, connecting us to the core of our being.

This gnosis isn't about escaping the abyss but about harnessing the strength to endure its depths, to learn from the darkness, and to emerge with a renewed sense of purpose and self. Campbell once observed, "The goal of life is to make your heartbeat match the beat of the universe, to match your nature with Nature," underscoring that gnosis is really about aligning our inner world with the universal truths.

Why should we live by dreams not our own? To blindly follow the visions of prophets without question is to tread a path paved by others, never discovering our own route or responding to our own call to adventure.

> Why tread the dreams of prophets, saints, long dead,
> When your own dream lies starved, unfed?
> Ezekiel's visions, Muhammad's divine plea,
> Yet where, oh seeker, is the dream for thee?

Campbell's urging to "follow your bliss" serves as a vibrant clarion call, encouraging us to seek what truly resonates with our soul, to chase after those dreams that are uniquely ours with courage and determination. It's in chasing our own dreams that we discover the unity we seek—not imposed from the outside but blossoming from within, born from reconciling all parts of ourselves, even those we fear or don't understand.

Step right up to the grand stage of life where prophets, sages, and thinkers of all stripes have trodden before us, each lighting up their path through their own dark nights of the soul. It's a dazzling show, with each luminary casting beams of wisdom that have weathered storms of doubt and despair. But here's the kicker—while their paths are illuminated under the spotlight, yours might just need a bit of a personal touch.

Sure, it's tempting to walk a path well-paved by giants. Their journeys are compelling, their victories hard-won, and their stories are there for the taking. But hold your horses! Grabbing their roadmap without adding your own splash of color, your own dash of experience? That's a fast track to feeling out of step with yourself. Before you know it, you're tuned into guilt—a truly crummy radio station, playing on the lowest frequency, guaranteed to bring you down.

Here's a thought: instead of pointing fingers, trying to sort the right from the wrong, why not use these titans as guides, not gospel? Draw from their wisdom, sure, but don't forget to stir in your own unique flavor. Develop your signature style in this life-dance through the lessons they've left behind and the fresh ones you pick up along the way.

So, let's grab the baton from these heroes and carve out trails that are unmistakably ours. It's not just about following footsteps; it's about dancing the steps to your own rhythm, leaving tracks that others might one day follow, adding their own moves as they go.

Unity, in its deepest sense, isn't about erasing differences but rather about the harmonious integration of our many facets. It's a dynamic balance that acknowledges both love and hate, seeing them as two sides of the same coin. Love drives us toward connection and unity, while hate—understood not as malice but as a passionate aversion—can ignite change, tearing down barriers that block our path to true unity with ourselves and the cosmos. Campbell eloquently said, "Love is a friendship set to music," inviting us to view the interplay of love and hate, chaos and order, as a symphony of human experience, leading us toward the ecstasy of being fully alive.

The metaphor of the orgasm, as the pinnacle of pleasure followed by a necessary return to equilibrium, captures the essence of life's ebb and flow. In this cycle of reaching for heights and returning to center, we discover the rhythm of existence itself. The quest for constant ecstasy is unsustainable, leading to annihilation; yet, it's in the balance—between striving and surrendering, ecstasy and tranquility—that we find true unity. This unity isn't about self-erasure but about dissolving the illusion of separation, revealing how interconnected everything truly is.

In our darkest moments, when vulnerability peeks through, we're invited to trust in the wisdom of our own journey, to maintain hope amid despair, and to believe in the transformative power of our inner light. Campbell reminds us, "Find a place inside where there's joy, and the joy will burn out the pain," pointing to the inner resources we have to navigate the abyss.

This journey through dark nights and cycles of love and hate is essentially about forging our personal myth, discovering a narrative that's solely ours, imbuing our existence with meaning and purpose. As we embrace this journey, we realize that the unity we seek isn't a far-off ideal but a vibrant, living reality, woven into the fabric of our being and the universe itself.

As we draw the curtains on our preface, let's hold onto a vital spark of wisdom: the dark night of the soul is not just an occasional visitor; it's an inevitable companion along the journey of life. Each of us, at one point or another—actually, probably several times over—will stroll through these stretches of shadow.

The march toward enlightenment, believe it or not, tends to handle itself. Whether we stride through with eyes wide open or stumble unknowingly, whether we cling to structured beliefs or carve our own wild paths, the universe has its way of nudging us toward that luminescent endpoint. And yes, that final glow might flicker into view in this lifetime or perhaps several reincarnations down the line.

You can, of course, put a little pep in your step with practices like meditation and yoga. These techniques aren't just exercises; they're opportunities to discover profound truths in the stillness of those challenging nights. These truths light up like fireflies, guiding us through future dark times and serving as beacons for those who will walk this path after us.

And then there's the sloth. In our relentless pursuit of enlightenment, let's not forget the wisdom of simply being. Sometimes, embracing the sloth's way—slowing down, being fully present, luxuriating in the art of doing nothing—is the highest form of enlightenment. In the words of Lao Tzu,

"Doing nothing is better than being busy doing nothing."

So, as we wrap up this preface, carry with you the light of those quiet moments, the slow and steady pace of the sloth, and the firefly truths that emerge in the dark. Let them illuminate your path and inspire others long after our tales are told. Here's to finding enlightenment, not by racing to the finish line, but by enjoying every step, every breath, every pause along the way.

The Path Ahead

The book is divided into three sections, each designed to guide you deeper into the mysteries of Hermetic wisdom, the nature of creation, and the alchemy of personal transformation.

- **Section 1: Hermetic Philosophy and Universal Truths**
  We begin by delving into the ancient teachings of Hermeticism, exploring its foundational principles, historical roots, and enduring relevance. Hermetic philosophy offers a map for understanding the interconnected nature of the cosmos and our place within it. Through these teachings, you'll discover how to unlock a deeper sense of purpose and harmony in your life.

- **Section 2: The Demiurge and the Hidden God**
  The second section introduces the enigmatic figure of the Demiurge, a creator of worlds and a central figure in many spiritual and philosophical traditions. We'll explore archetypes and symbolism, tools that bridge the conscious and subconscious realms, enabling us to grasp the profound forces shaping our reality. By understanding these symbols, you'll uncover new ways to interpret and engage with the mysteries of existence.

- **Section 3: Alchemical Training for Mental Transmutations**
  The final section invites you to become the alchemist of your own mind, transforming limiting beliefs into empowering truths. Drawing upon the Hermetic principle of "As within, so without," you'll learn how to use affirmations and other tools to align your subconscious with your highest aspirations. This is the art of mental alchemy—a practical, transformative practice that empowers you to shape your destiny from the inside out.

This book is a call to action, inviting you to explore Hermetic wisdom, archetypes, and mental alchemy to awaken your inner magick. Let its teachings illuminate your path to self-discovery and profound connection with the universe.

Ode to the Inner Adventurer

Oh, the inner worlds we tread,
Spun of dreams and woven thread;
Beneath the surface calm, a sea,
Where shadows dance and spirits free.

With a laugh, we leap and bound,
Where whispers of our soul resound;
Through the maze that twists within,
Each twist and turn, a chance to win.

"Follow your bliss!" the old maps say,
Marking trails in a playful way;
Through the dark and stormy night,
Guided by our inner light.

The cave we fear, so dark and deep,
Holds the treasures that we seek;
With courage clasped in trembling hands,
We explore these strange new lands.

A lighthearted skip in every step,
Through emotional depths, we've wept;
In this journey, the heart's true art,
Reveals the parts of our own heart.

So, brave explorer, have no fear,
The chaos is welcome here;
With joy as compass, love as chart,
Set sail to map your hidden heart.

In laughter, find the strength to face
Each shadowed corner, each tight space;
For in this path, though we roam,
Every twist and turn leads home.

Section I

Divine Alignment: Let the Magick Begin

Introduction

The ancient wisdom from the Temple of Delphi reminds us of a profound truth:

"Know thyself, and thou shalt know the universe and God."

This declaration encapsulates an age-old quest for deeper understanding and self-realization. A quest for understanding not just the material world, but the very fabric of reality itself. This book aims to take you on an exploration into one of the most enigmatic and profound sets of ideas known as Hermetic Philosophy.

The principles of Hermeticism are neither new nor part of some ephemeral trend; they're as old as the quest for wisdom itself. Rooted in antiquity, these ideas have survived the passage of time, permeating various disciplines like philosophy, science, and spirituality. Hermeticism transcends cultural, religious, and geographical boundaries, resonating with seekers who are drawn to the enigmatic nature of existence.

What is Hermetic Philosophy?

Hermetic Philosophy refers to a set of spiritual, philosophical, and esoteric teachings attributed to **Hermes Trismegistus**, an ancient figure who is said to be the fusion of the Greek god Hermes and the Egyptian god Thoth. This school of thought encompasses a range of ideas that are primarily concerned with the nature of divinity, the cosmos, the human soul, and the intricate interconnections among them.

The All and The Principle of Mentalism

As the great Hermetic text "The Kybalion" proclaims,

"The All is Mind; The Universe is Mental."

This simple yet profound statement serves as the cornerstone of Hermetic thought. It asserts that the universe is not a mere collection of random, disconnected events but a vast, interconnected web of mental energy. You, as an individual, are a microcosm of this grand, infinite macrocosm. By understanding yourself—your soul, mind, and spirit—you can gain insights into the Universe and the Divine.

A Map for the Seeker

This book is designed as a guide for those who have found themselves at the doorstep of Hermetic philosophy, perhaps through intuition, life circumstances, or an insatiable thirst for knowledge. We will journey through the core principles of Hermeticism, explore its rich historical context, and delve into its practical applications for modern life. It aims to be more than a mere overview but an initiatory experience, aiding you in the quest to align your soul with the Divine, and live a life of greater wisdom, understanding, and inner peace.

Why This Book?

The journey towards self-discovery and spiritual enlightenment is often filled with challenges, doubts, and countless questions. While Hermeticism doesn't claim to offer all the answers, it provides a robust framework that encourages you to ask better questions, seek deeper truths, and gain a more holistic understanding of yourself and the Universe. Through the course of this book, we'll unravel these complex ideas in a manner that is both accessible to the beginner and enriching for those already acquainted with esoteric teachings.

As it is said by Socrates,

"The unexamined life is not worth living."

Therefore, let this book serve as a catalyst for your personal examination, inspiring you to delve deeper into your being, beyond the material world, and closer to the essence of who you truly are.

What Lies Ahead

Each chapter of this book focuses on a unique facet of Hermetic philosophy, interwoven with practical applications, historical context, and thought-provoking quotes from figures of wisdom throughout the ages. Whether you are a seeker, a skeptic, or simply curious, this book aspires to engage your mind, touch your soul, and ignite your spirit.

Objective of the Book

Baba Dioum, a Senegalese forestry engineer, astutely observed:

> "In the end, we will conserve only what we love; we will love only what we understand and we will understand only what we are taught."

His words emphasize the crucial role of education in nurturing both love and comprehension. Such wisdom rings true for our journey through the labyrinth of Hermetic philosophy.

Why Hermeticism?

The modern world, despite its advancements, leaves many of us feeling disconnected—from ourselves, from others, and from the spiritual or divine. Hermetic philosophy offers an alternative lens through which we can perceive and understand the world, providing intellectual and spiritual tools to forge a deeper connection with the universe and our place within it.

The Book's Promise

The core objective of this book is to serve as both a primer and a guide for your journey into the world of Hermetic wisdom. It aims to present complex esoteric principles in a manner that is accessible to the lay reader, while also offering depth and additional avenues of exploration for those already familiar with these concepts.

Beyond Theoretical Understanding

While the book provides a comprehensive understanding of Hermetic principles, its objectives go beyond mere intellectual comprehension. As said by Carl Jung,

> "Knowledge rests not upon truth alone, but upon error also."

The book seeks to challenge your existing perceptions and encourage you to experience these principles in your daily life, thus aiming for an experiential understanding that transcends theoretical knowledge.

Aiding Personal Transformation

Another key objective is to assist you in applying Hermetic wisdom in your personal journey towards transformation. By the end of this book, you should be equipped with practical tools to enhance your sense of well-being, find a greater purpose, and align your soul with its divine essence.

Empowering the Seeker

The book aims to empower you, the reader, by offering you the keys to unlock your own innate wisdom. Hermetic philosophy teaches that the answers you seek are already within you; this book serves as a guide to help you find those answers and unlock your true potential.

Creating a Global Dialogue

Finally, the objective is not just individual but collective. We are at a pivotal moment in human history, where the decisions we make will have repercussions for generations to come. By fostering a deeper understanding of Hermetic principles, this book aims to contribute to a broader dialogue about spirituality, morality, and the interconnectedness of all things, in the hope that this will lead to a more harmonious, sustainable world.

Dive into these pages, not just to read, but to awaken. Let each word be a gentle nudge towards a new horizon—a fresh way of seeing, feeling, and existing within the cosmos. Embrace this book not just as learning but as a profound initiation, an unfolding journey that leads us into the heart of Hermetic wisdom.

Know this: the absolute reality, that profound mystery, is beyond our mere comprehension. It cannot be captured in words but is rather felt in quiet moments of reflection. Anything that distances you from love steers you away from the divine. Love freely, without judgment—embrace yourself and others in their entirety. And remember, as Rumi whispered,

"Silence is the language of God, all else is poor translation."

Let us then begin our humble attempt to translate the ineffable.

Foundations of Hermetic Philosophy

The Origins and Influences

Drawing from the teachings of Hermes Trismegistus, the maxim

"As above, so below; as within, so without"

captures the core of Hermetic philosophy, resonating with seekers, mystics, and scholars through the ages. But where did Hermeticism originate, and what are the currents that fed into its stream of thought?

The Fabled Hermes Trismegistus

Hermes Trismegistus, or "Thrice-Greatest Hermes," is the figure to whom the origins of Hermeticism are traditionally attributed. He is considered a fusion of the Greek god Hermes and the Egyptian god Thoth, both deities of wisdom and communication. While the historicity of Hermes Trismegistus is a subject of scholarly debate, his influence on the Hermetic tradition is indisputable.

Ancient Egypt: The Cradle of Hermeticism

Hermeticism is deeply rooted in the ancient Egyptian worldview, particularly in the traditions of alchemy, astrology, and theurgy (ritual magic). The Egyptians were pioneers in exploring the metaphysical aspects of existence, and their religious and philosophical ideas laid the groundwork for what would later be formalized as Hermetic principles.

The Greek Philosophical Influence

While Egypt provided the foundational religious and mystical elements, Greek philosophical thought, particularly through Neoplatonism, also played a critical role. Neoplatonism introduced ideas such as the hierarchical structure of reality and the notion of an ultimate, unknowable source, aspects which were later integrated into Hermetic doctrine.

The Gnostic Connection

Gnosticism, a religious and philosophical movement that emphasizes direct, personal experience of the Divine, has noticeable parallels with Hermeticism. Both traditions speak of a higher, more real spiritual realm and espouse the idea of gnosis, or direct spiritual knowledge, as the path to enlightenment.

The Renaissance Revival

The European Renaissance saw a revival of Hermetic philosophy, largely due to the translation of Hermetic texts like the "Corpus Hermeticum" into Latin. Renaissance thinkers like Marsilio Ficino and Giovanni Pico della Mirandola incorporated Hermetic ideas into their work, blending them with Christian mysticism and the emerging currents of humanism and natural science.

The Influence of Kabbalah

The Kabbalistic tradition of Judaism, particularly its focus on the emanative structure of the divine realm and its method of textual interpretation, has also found echoes in Hermetic thought. Both traditions share the idea of a hidden wisdom, accessible only to the initiated.

Modern Interpretations

In modern times, Hermetic principles have been adopted and adapted by various esoteric movements, including Theosophy, the New Thought movement, and various branches of contemporary paganism and New Age philosophy. Authors like Aleister Crowley and institutions like the Hermetic Order of the Golden Dawn have kept Hermeticism alive in various forms, ensuring its relevance in contemporary spiritual discourse.

As it is said by Isaac Newton,

> "If I have seen further it is by standing on the shoulders of Giants."

The Hermetic philosophy is a foundational bedrock that has informed and influenced a rich array of religious, philosophical, and mystical traditions throughout history. From ancient wisdom to Renaissance thought and modern interpretations, its principles have been echoed, expanded upon, and integrated into diverse spiritual paths.

By delving into its foundational roots and the myriad traditions it has touched, we gain a profound appreciation for the vastness and intricacy of Hermeticism, deepening our exploration of its enlightening teachings.

The Basic Principles

The ancient Greek philosopher Sophocles once stated,

"To know nothing is the happiest life,"

highlighting the simplicity of ignorance. However, the seekers of Hermetic wisdom would ardently disagree. For them, the pursuit of knowledge and understanding provides not just happiness, but the key to spiritual enlightenment and self-mastery. Here, we delve into the basic principles that constitute the foundation of Hermetic thought.

The Principle of Mentalism

"The All is Mind; The Universe is Mental,"

This statement comes from foundational texts of Hermetic philosophy. At its core, the phrase refers to "the All" as the ultimate, infinite, and all-encompassing source or Divine force behind everything. Think of "the All" as the universal consciousness or supreme entity from which all existence springs.

The principle posits that everything in existence is a manifestation of Mind. Hence, by understanding the nature of Mind, we can grasp the nature of reality. Mentalism implies that the power of thought is paramount in comprehending existence.

The aphorism "The All is Mind; The Universe is Mental" accentuates the idea that everything, from vast galaxies to minute particles, emerges from and is steered by this universal consciousness or mind. In essence, the entirety of reality is birthed from thought or mental energy.

The Principle of Correspondence

"As above, so below; as below, so above."

This principle suggests that there is a harmony and correspondence between the various planes of existence — physical, mental, and spiritual. Understanding the laws that govern one plane can aid in understanding the laws that govern the others.

The statement "As above, so below; as below, so above" signifies that there is a harmony, agreement, or correspondence between the physical, terrestrial realm (the "below") and the spiritual, cosmic realm (the "above"). In essence, it conveys that patterns found on one level of reality (such as the physical world) can also be found on other levels, whether they be mental, spiritual, or cosmic. It's a concept that suggests the microcosm reflects the macrocosm, and vice versa.

The Principle of Vibration

"Nothing rests; everything moves; everything vibrates."

According to this principle, all things in the universe, from the largest celestial body to the tiniest particle, are in a constant state of vibration. This principle explains the differences between different manifestations of matter and energy.

The phrase "Nothing rests; everything moves; everything vibrates" underscores the idea that at the most fundamental level, everything in the universe is in a state of constant motion and vibration. Whether it's atoms, molecules, or galaxies, nothing is truly static. Everything, from the tiniest particle to vast cosmic structures, is vibrating at its own unique frequency. This principle highlights the dynamic and ever-changing nature of existence.

The Principle of Polarity

"Everything is dual; everything has poles; everything has its pair of opposites."

This principle describes the duality inherent in all things. Light and darkness, hot and cold, love and hate—these are all examples of polar opposites that are simply different degrees on a spectrum.

The statement "Everything is dual; everything has poles; everything has its pair of opposites" speaks to the innate duality present in all facets of existence. This duality doesn't necessarily signify opposition in a combative sense but rather describes complementary forces or states that often exist on a spectrum. Light and dark, hot and cold, positive and negative—these are all examples of polar opposites that are simply different degrees on a spectrum.

For instance, consider temperature: hot and cold are not separate, isolated states but rather points on a continuous scale. The same goes for light and dark, where varying degrees of lightness or darkness blend into each other. This principle of polarity highlights that what might appear as conflicting or opposite forces can also be viewed as two extremes of a single continuum. Understanding this principle encourages us to see the interconnectedness and relativity of seemingly opposite states or conditions. Instead of viewing the world in black and white, it teaches us to recognize the shades of gray in between, fostering a more holistic and interconnected understanding of the universe.

The Principle of Rhythm

"Everything flows, out and in; everything has its tides; all things rise and fall."

This principle explains that there is a rhythm to the cycles of nature and life. Understanding the rhythm can help us anticipate and prepare for the ebbs and flows of life's circumstances.

The phrase "Everything flows, out and in; everything has its tides; all things rise and fall" reflects the principle of rhythm in the universe. Everything, from emotions to natural phenomena, moves in cycles. It's a reminder that life has its ebbs and flows, peaks and valleys, and that change and cyclicity are inherent parts of existence.

The Principle of Cause and Effect

"Every cause has its effect; every effect has its cause."

Nothing happens by chance; there is a reason for every event and a consequence for every action. By understanding the cause and effect relationships that govern our world, we can become masters of our fate.

The statement "Every cause has its effect; every effect has its cause" encapsulates the idea of causality. It means that nothing happens by chance; there's a reason behind every event, and every event will subsequently lead to another. It emphasizes the interconnectedness and sequence of events, suggesting that actions have consequences, and those consequences become the causes of further events.

The Principle of Gender

"Gender is in everything; everything has its masculine and feminine principles."

This principle is not limited to sexual or biological differences but extends to mental and spiritual aspects as well. The harmonious interaction between the masculine and feminine energies is essential for creation and balance.

The statement "Gender is in everything; everything has its masculine and feminine principles" emphasizes the omnipresence of both masculine and feminine energies across the universe. While not strictly tied to biological definitions, these energies represent varying qualities and attributes.

Masculine energy often embodies action, logic, and assertiveness, while feminine energy resonates with intuition, receptivity, and nurturing. However, these energies aren't rigid binaries but exist along a spectrum, fluidly interplaying and combining in diverse ways in nature and existence. The principle underscores the essential balance and harmony achieved when both energies are acknowledged and integrated.

Drawing from the wisdom of antiquity, Pythagoras proclaimed,

"The beginning is the half of the whole."

Understanding these foundational principles is the first step towards mastering Hermetic philosophy. These principles provide the framework for our exploration of the universe, self, and the divine. They serve as guideposts on the path to enlightenment, aiding us in our quest to transcend the limitations of material existence.

Beyond the tangible and material lies a realm of the intangible, the spiritual. In Hermetic philosophy, the material world we perceive with our senses is but one half of existence. This world, with its physicality and transience, is bound by duality: day and night, joy and sorrow, life and death. Such duality serves as a constant reminder of the limitations and contrasts inherent in the material plane.

In Hermetic philosophy, our material world is interconnected with a higher spiritual realm. Think of the two as reflections of each other. While the material world is characterized by duality and contrasts, the spiritual realm represents unity and wholeness. To grow spiritually is to recognize and nurture our connection with this higher realm, ultimately understanding and embodying the divine essence that exists within all of us.

The journey of Hermetic practice, then, is about navigating and transcending this duality. By understanding and harmonizing with the principles of the universe, the seeker aims to rise above the material confines, moving ever closer to pure consciousness and unity with the divine. This ascent is not a rejection of the material but an embrace of a more expansive, holistic understanding of existence, where the soul recognizes its true nature and potential.

This forms the crux of what is meant by the Basic Principles in Hermetic philosophy—a key to unlocking a universe of potential within and around us.

The Concept of the All or God

Echoing timeless wisdom from the Bhagavad Gita, the ancient scripture reveals,

"Man is made by his belief. As he believes, so he is."

In Hermetic philosophy, the concept of the All or God is crucial for shaping our beliefs, guiding our actions, and understanding the Universe itself. But what exactly does Hermeticism teach us about this ultimate source of existence?

The All is Ineffable

In Hermetic philosophy, "the All" refers to the omnipresent, all-encompassing Divine or God, which is the source of everything in existence. Though we can strive to understand it, connect with it, and discuss its manifestations, the true essence of the All remains beyond the full grasp of the human mind.

It's a profound Mystery, a limitless expanse of Divine Intelligence. While seekers of wisdom can journey towards a deeper comprehension and connection with this Divine, its complete essence remains eternally elusive, perpetually inviting us to explore and understand more.

Hermeticism asserts that the All, or the source of everything, is beyond full human comprehension. While it can be approximated, discussed, and even experienced in some form, it cannot be wholly defined or understood by the human mind. In this sense, the All exists as a Mystery, forever inviting the seeker into a deeper understanding but never fully revealing its essence.

The All as the Universal Mind

Central to the Hermetic philosophy is the understanding of the All, often envisioned as the Universal Mind. This isn't merely an abstract concept; instead, it's an attempt to conceptualize the most profound, infinite, and omnipresent intelligence in existence.

Imagine the Universal Mind as an infinite library that contains every thought ever thought and every action ever performed. It's not just a storage but a dynamic field where information is continuously added, accessed, and interconnected. Beyond just knowledge, this Universal Mind is the very source of energy and power. Every spark of inspiration, every intuition, and every force of nature is derived from this omnipotent Mind.

Moreover, the Universal Mind isn't static. It's more like a vast, interconnected network, where each node represents a thought or action. When we think or act, we're not just adding to this network but also influencing its overall configuration. Every decision, every emotion, and every realization sends ripples through this intricate web.

Our individual minds are but reflections of this grand Universal Mind. When we think or act, it's not in isolation. Our thoughts and actions echo in the vastness of the Universal Mind, impacting the collective consciousness. It's a dynamic interplay, where the part affects the whole, and the whole influences the part.

In embracing this perspective, we realize that our existence is deeply interconnected. Our inner world and the vast external universe are reflections of each other, both manifestations of the Universal Mind's boundless expanse.

In Hermetic philosophy, while the Universal Mind is a central concept, it is not equivalent to The All, which is beyond human comprehension. Instead, practitioners are encouraged to be vigilant of their thoughts and feelings, observing them without judgment. This mindful observation fosters a deeper awareness and connection to the Universal Mind, aligning one's inner self with the greater, incomprehensible expanse of The All.

Panentheism and the All

The Hermetic view of the All provides a nuanced understanding of the nature of divinity that aligns with the panentheistic worldview. In panentheism, there's a delicate balance that's struck between seeing the Divine in everything and yet understanding that the Divine also transcends everything. Let's unpack this.

Imagine the universe as an ever-expanding canvas filled with intricate patterns, colors, and forms. Every star, planet, living being, and even inanimate objects are brushstrokes on this canvas. In pantheism, this canvas, in its entirety, is God. Every brushstroke, every pattern is a part of God.

However, Hermeticism, with its panentheistic leanings, adds another dimension to this perception. It proposes that while every brushstroke on the canvas is an expression of the Divine, the true essence of the Divine isn't confined to just the canvas. The artist who wields the brush, the inspiration behind every stroke, the very essence that gives life to the canvas, exists beyond it. This artist—this force—is the All.

So, while everything within our perceptual reality is an expression and manifestation of the All, the All itself is not limited by this reality. It permeates every nook and cranny, animating the universe with its presence, but it also exists beyond, in realms and dimensions that our human faculties can't fully grasp.

This understanding brings a profound sense of reverence for both the seen and the unseen, the known and the mysterious. It's a recognition that while we can find the Divine in the world around us, there's always an infinite depth to the Divine that remains beyond our comprehension.

The All as a Field of Potentialities

The All is not just a cosmic entity but also a field of infinite potentialities. It is from this boundless sea of potential that all forms manifest. By aligning our minds with the Universal Mind, Hermetic practitioners believe they can tap into these potentialities, bringing forth healing, wisdom, and transformative experiences.

The notion of the All as a "Field of Potentialities" offers a fresh and dynamic way to contemplate the nature of existence. Much like an endless ocean with depths unseen, the All encompasses both the manifested and the yet-to-manifest, the known and the yet-to-be-known. This view doesn't just see the universe as a static creation, but as a living, breathing entity, forever unfolding from the infinite wellspring of potential that the All represents.

When we say "potentialities," we refer to the possibilities that are yet to take form, like seeds in the ground awaiting the right conditions to sprout. They are not voids or absences; rather, they're vibrant energies, ready to be actualized. The universe, in this view, is in a continuous state of becoming, emerging from the All's reservoir of possibilities.

Now, what does this mean for the individual? If all of existence arises from this profound depth of potential, then each of us, too, is born from and carries within us a piece of this limitless potential. This realization is both empowering and humbling. It suggests that our true nature is not confined to our physical form and the limitations of our ego, but is intrinsically linked to the vastness of the All.

Hermetic practitioners, with their deep understanding of these concepts, strive to align themselves with this Universal Mind. They believe that by resonating with its frequencies, they can access its treasures. This isn't just about material gains or superficial powers. It's about deeper healing, gaining profound wisdom, and experiencing transformations that align them more closely with their true, divine nature. By tuning into this infinite field of potentialities, they aspire to bring into their lives and the lives of others the very best that the universe has to offer.

The Principle of Correspondence in Understanding the All

The Hermetic adage "As above, so below" applies here too. Understanding the All is not just a cosmic endeavor but an inward journey as well. The All is mirrored in each one of us, making each individual a unique expression of the Divine.

The Principle of Correspondence is foundational in Hermetic thought, holding that there's a harmonious relationship between the various levels of existence, both seen and unseen. When we say "As above, so below," we are referring to this mirrored relationship between the vast cosmos and the microcosm of individual existence.

While the All might be envisioned as this vast, unfathomable expanse, it is also present in the very intricacies of our being. Think of it as a hologram, where every part contains the whole. Each individual, in their essence, carries the entirety of the All within. This is not to say we are all-powerful or all-knowing, but that the essence, the blueprint of the Divine, is imprinted within us.

This correspondence implies a profound truth: by understanding ourselves, by diving deep into our psyche, emotions, and even our physical bodies, we can glean insights about the nature of the All. The reverse is also true. By understanding the larger universal principles, we can better navigate our personal lives. It establishes a feedback loop of understanding; the microcosm informs our understanding of the macrocosm and vice versa.

For those on a spiritual journey, this principle provides a path of exploration. By meditating, reflecting, and introspecting, one can touch the edges of the All within. Every insight gained, every moment of clarity, is not just personal illumination but a step closer to grasping the vastness of the All.

Moreover, this interconnectedness has ethical implications. If we are each a reflection of the Divine, it calls for a deep respect and reverence for all life forms. It instills a sense of responsibility, urging us to treat every individual as a manifestation of the Divine, recognizing the sacredness in each being. This perspective shifts our approach to life, encouraging compassion, understanding, and unity.

Divine Will and Human Will

In the Hermetic perspective, human will and divine will are not mutually exclusive but intertwined. When a person aligns their will with the Divine, they are not surrendering their agency but rather fulfilling their highest potential. In doing so, they act as a co-creator with the All.

Divine Will is the underlying force that drives the universe towards harmony, balance, and evolution. It is the unsung rhythm that ensures stars burn, planets orbit, and seasons change. More than just these tangible manifestations, Divine Will also propels spiritual growth, the expansion of consciousness, and the realization of the divine essence in all beings.

Humans, distinct in their possession of consciousness and self-awareness, hold a singular gift – the power of choice. This ability to choose, to act and react, forms the crux of human will. Yet, this gift isn't an isolated trait; it's an extension of the divine, granted to allow humans to chart their journey of growth, exploration, and evolution.

When one becomes aware of this higher intent, recognizing the grand blueprint of existence, a beautiful synchronicity between personal desires and the universe's direction becomes evident. This understanding heralds the alignment of one's will with the divine. It isn't about abandoning personal desires or ambitions but refining them to harmonize with a more magnificent purpose.

When this alignment occurs, the individual experiences a profound resonance. Decisions and actions taken from this congruence reverberate deeply, influencing not just the individual but the very fabric of the cosmos. These aligned actions generate positive change, healing, and growth for both the individual and their surroundings.

Furthermore, in this harmonized state, the individual becomes a co-creator, echoing a crucial Hermetic belief. This role stresses collaboration with the Divine rather than mere subjugation. Acting from this place of alignment means harnessing personal energies and tapping into the vast cosmic reservoir. In doing so, individuals become Divine instruments, helping actualize its vision in the material realm.

In essence, the alignment of human will with Divine Will is a transformative journey. It beckons individuals to recognize their potential beyond just their physical existence, highlighting their role as spiritual beings interlaced into the expansive fabric of the cosmos.

The Concept of Unity and Separation

The idea of unity and separation is a cornerstone in many philosophical and spiritual traditions, and Hermeticism is no exception. At the heart of this perspective is the intricate dance between oneness and multiplicity.

Imagine an unbroken expanse of water – vast, deep, and serene. This is the All in its undifferentiated state, a boundless continuum of existence. Within this expanse, however, are currents, waves, ripples, and vortices, each appearing distinct and separate. They are born from the water, live as the water, and eventually subside back into it. These transient forms are like the myriad manifestations of the universe – galaxies, stars, planets, living beings, thoughts, emotions, and even concepts. While they appear separate, their essence is the same. They are all expressions of that vast water body.

In our everyday experience, we often get entangled with these transient forms, identifying with our bodies, minds, emotions, roles, and possessions. We define ourselves by our relationships, jobs, successes, failures, dreams, and fears. This identification creates a sense of separation – from others, from the world, and even from the Divine. It's as if each wave on the ocean thinks it exists in isolation, forgetting it is part of the vast sea.

Hermeticism teaches that this sense of separation is an illusion, often referred to as "maya" in other traditions. It is a necessary illusion, for it allows for the play of existence, the drama of life, and the journey of the soul. But it is an illusion nonetheless.

The path of the Hermetic practitioner, then, is to pierce through this veil of separateness. Through meditation, contemplation, and various esoteric practices, the seeker strives to experience their intrinsic connection with everything. It's a shift in perspective – from seeing oneself as a solitary wave to recognizing one's essence as the water itself.

When this realization dawns, a profound transformation occurs. The barriers that once seemed so real – between self and other, between humanity and nature, between the individual and the Divine – start to dissolve. Compassion, understanding, and universal love arise naturally, for one sees oneself in all and all in oneself.

This concept of unity amidst apparent separation is not just a philosophical musing. It's a living truth, waiting to be realized. And as the Hermetic axiom goes,

> "Know thyself, and thou shalt know all the mysteries of the gods and of the universe."

The journey from separation to unity, from illusion to truth, is a journey inward, towards one's true nature and the heart of existence.

As Lao Tzu eloquently put it,

> "The Tao that can be told is not the eternal Tao; the name that can be named is not the eternal name."

In the Hermetic tradition, the All is the infinite source from which all emanates. But, much like Lao Tzu's description of the Tao, the true nature of the All surpasses human comprehension and language. The ancient Hermetic texts teach that while the All is within everything and everyone, it is a grave mistake to believe that we, in our limited human forms, can claim its totality. It is a reminder of humility and the limitations of human understanding.

Think of the All as the vast, uncharted ocean. While a drop of water contains the same essence as the ocean, it would be a mistake for the drop to claim it is the entire ocean. Similarly, while the Divine spark is within each of us, making us intrinsic parts of the grand cosmic design, we are not the entirety of the All. Our individual consciousness, with its thoughts, emotions, and perceptions, is but a fleeting wave on the vast expanse of the Universal Mind.

The journey in Hermeticism, then, is not about becoming gods or claiming divine omniscience. Instead, it is about realizing our profound connection with the All, understanding our place within the cosmic scheme, and striving to align our lives with higher principles. This alignment brings about wisdom, harmony, and enlightenment.

While the All remains a mystery, its essence can be felt, its principles can be understood, and its wisdom can be channeled. But the complete knowledge and essence of the All? That remains beyond human grasp, a reminder of the eternal dance between the known and the unknown, between seeking and surrendering.

It's vital for seekers on the Hermetic path to approach the teachings with humility. In recognizing our limitations, we open ourselves to greater truths and deeper experiences. The Hermetic quest is not about attaining divine status but about understanding our divine connection. It's a journey of unfolding, of becoming more attuned to the rhythms of the cosmos, and of realizing our potential within the grand fabric of existence.

Let me give you the key:

What other people think is none of your business, and what you think of yourself is also none of your business. Remove all the masks, just breathe, and observe yourself without judgment. Each split within yourself has a different personality—just observe them.

Breathe and be present where you are; you are exactly where you are supposed to be. By breathing and being present, you align with the divine will. Practice patience, relaxation, acceptance, and allow the divine will to manifest through you.

Absolute simplicity is found in just being, recognizing that endings and beginnings are two sides of the same coin. You are not merely a thinking machine but a knowing machine—go beyond words. Observe what your mind is selling you; what you think of yourself is none of your business.

Can you love every particle in the universe, including yourself, with pure love? Once you do, you will achieve true enlightenment. You are beyond any idea. Breathe, enter within yourself, and serve the manifestation of the divine. If you want to understand, observe nature and how it works. Relax, for you are already there.

The Tripartite Model of Humans

Body, Soul, and Spirit

The transcendentalist thinker, Ralph Waldo Emerson, penned the evocative line,

"Every man is a divinity in disguise."

This sentiment encapsulates the profound depth and potential within each individual. To understand this hidden divinity, Hermetic philosophy offers a tripartite model of humans as an amalgamation of body, soul, and spirit. Let's delve into what each component signifies and how they interact.

The Body: The Physical Vessel

The ancient "Corpus Hermeticum," a cornerstone of Hermetic philosophy, proclaims,

"Man is a divine being, and for him the body is not a permanent dwelling, but only a temporary abode."

In this grand existence, where multiple realms and dimensions intertwine, the body occupies a unique position. It anchors us to the earthly plane, giving us the means to experience, learn from, and interact with the material world around us. It's through our physical senses – sight, touch, taste, hearing, and smell – that we gather information, process emotions, and form perceptions.

This physical existence, however, is not an end in itself. Instead, it serves as a conduit, facilitating the soul's journey towards alignment with the spirit and the divine. While our skin, bones, and organs provide the framework for our earthly experiences, it's essential to understand that they are temporary. They are tools, in a sense, designed for the grander purpose of spiritual exploration and evolution.

But even as the body is transient, it is sacred. Every heartbeat, every breath, and every sensation is a testament to the life force that animates it. It's a constant reminder of the intricate balance between the seen and the unseen, the physical and the metaphysical.

The Hermetic tradition emphasizes this duality. By understanding the body as both a physical entity and a vessel for higher consciousness, practitioners are encouraged to honor, nurture, and care for it. It becomes more than just a vehicle for daily tasks; it is the temple that houses the divine essence of the soul and spirit.

Hence, the body's health and well-being are not just matters of physical fitness but are deeply entwined with one's spiritual journey. By harmonizing the body with the soul and spirit, one sets the stage for a deeper understanding and realization of the mysteries of existence.

The Soul: The Eternal Essence

The English novelist Daniel Defoe insightfully remarked,

> "The soul is placed in the body like a rough diamond, and must be polished, or the luster of it will never appear."

The soul stands as the intermediary between the physical body and the ethereal spirit, acting as a bridge between the tangible and the intangible. While the body is bound by the limitations of the physical realm, the soul, being less constrained, flits between the material and the spiritual, bringing depth to our earthly experiences.

Every joy, sorrow, love, and heartbreak; every dream and aspiration; they all reside within the soul. It is this part of us that feels the pangs of nostalgia, the yearnings for something more, and the pull towards understanding the mysteries of existence. Each experience we go through, be it painful or pleasurable, imprints itself onto the soul, shaping its evolution.

Moreover, it's through the soul that we express our individuality. Everyone has a unique soul signature, a distinct blend of desires, fears, and inclinations. This signature is what differentiates one person from another, giving rise to the vast diversity of human personalities and behaviors.

But the soul is not just a passive receiver. It is also an active participant in the journey of life. With its free will, it makes choices, forges paths, and determines how to react to various situations. These choices and reactions, in turn, influence the soul's growth and development. Some paths lead to wisdom and enlightenment, while others might lead to lessons learned the hard way.

The prominent theosophist, Annie Besant, proclaimed,

"Evolution is the law of life, and the soul is no exception."

In the grand cosmic narrative, the soul's journey is one of return. Having emanated from a source of pure consciousness, it strives, through cycles of experiences and lifetimes, to return to this source. The challenges, triumphs, and lessons along the way are but stepping stones in this homeward journey. By understanding its nature and purpose, we can better navigate the complexities of life, aligning our actions with the higher goals of soul evolution and spiritual awakening.

The renowned Swiss psychiatrist, Carl Jung, astutely observed,

"Until you make the unconscious conscious, it will direct your life, and you will call it fate."

In the Hermetic view, the soul's role in spiritual evolution is akin to making the unconscious conscious, shedding light on the deepest recesses of our being and steering us toward our ultimate fate: unity with the All. It is the soul that navigates this intricate maze, learning, growing, and ultimately evolving into a higher state of being.

The Spirit: The Divine Spark

The spirit exists beyond the confines of personal identity and earthly attachments. While the body is tied to the physical realm and the soul navigates the realm of emotions, desires, and thoughts, the spirit operates in the realm of pure consciousness and universal connection. It's untainted by the fluctuations of human experiences and remains a constant source of inner light and guidance.

In many ways, the spirit represents our truest essence. It's the core of our being, the eternal aspect of ourselves that was never born and will never die. It carries the memory of our divine origin and holds the blueprint for our ultimate purpose. It is this spiritual core that gives life to both the body and the soul, energizing them with a life force that animates our entire existence.

Where the soul might get entangled in the challenges and dramas of life, the spirit maintains a bird's-eye view, seeing beyond the immediacy of present circumstances to the vast continuum of existence. This is why, during moments of deep introspection or meditation, individuals often receive insights and wisdom that seem beyond their personal understanding. It's the spirit communicating, offering guidance from a higher vantage point.

This divine spark within us constantly nudges us towards our higher selves. It instills in us a sense of wonder about the universe, a drive to understand the mysteries of existence, and a yearning to connect with something greater than ourselves. It's the source of those inexplicable moments of awe we feel when gazing at a starry sky, the profound peace experienced in deep meditation, or the overwhelming love that can surge within us without any apparent reason.

To truly understand oneself, it is essential to recognize and nurture this spiritual aspect. For it is through the spirit that we reconnect with the All, merging our individual consciousness with the Universal Mind. This union, the ultimate goal of many spiritual paths, brings about a profound sense of peace, wholeness, and enlightenment, as the individual realizes their oneness with all of existence.

The Interactions Between the Triad

Body and Soul

The body, the tangible representation of our existence, mirrors the conditions of the soul. The soul, capturing the myriad experiences of life, influences the body's state. When the soul rejoices, the body responds with vitality, and conversely, when the soul is burdened, the body might exhibit signs of weariness or ailment. This interplay between the body and soul is palpable in everyday experiences. Phrases like, "I feel heavy-hearted," are more than just poetic expressions—they hint at how deeply our emotional and mental states can affect our physical well-being.

The soul, on the other hand, is shaped and molded by our experiences in the physical world. Every touch, taste, sight, and sound gets imprinted on the soul, adding layers to its depth. It's the reason why certain scents can evoke deep-seated memories or why a song can instantly transport us back to a moment in the past. These sensory experiences feed the soul, enabling it to grow and evolve.

The profound connection between body and soul is evident in the realm of health. Emotional trauma, suppressed feelings, and unprocessed experiences can manifest as physical ailments. Stress, for instance, isn't just a state of mind. Chronic stress can lead to a weakened immune system, heart disease, and other health complications. Conversely, physical ailments or imbalances can also impact our emotional and mental state, leading to feelings of depression, anxiety, or unease.

In Hermetic practices, understanding this intricate relationship is key. By treating the body as a sacred vessel and the soul as its divine inhabitant, one can work towards achieving a state of equilibrium. This involves not just physical exercises or dietary regulations but also meditative practices, emotional healing, and mental exercises.

When both body and soul are in harmony, it creates a conducive environment for the spirit to express itself. This is akin to tuning a musical instrument perfectly, allowing for the purest notes to be played. In such a state, the individual becomes more receptive to spiritual insights, guidance, and enlightenment. It's no wonder then that many ancient Hermetic teachings emphasize the importance of balance and harmony in all things, starting with the self.

Soul and Spirit

The soul, being deeply enmeshed in the human experience, is often swayed by desires, fears, and the myriad complexities of life. It carries the burdens of past experiences, memories, and karmic ties, all of which shape its perceptions and choices. At times, the soul can feel lost, clouded by its own accumulated baggage and the ever-present chaos of the material world.

The spirit, in contrast, remains untainted by these earthly experiences. It stands as a beacon of pure, divine energy, radiating wisdom, love, and a deep understanding of the cosmic order. It is the unchanging essence that remains constant, even as the soul undergoes various transformations through lifetimes. While the soul may forget its true nature amid life's tempests, the spirit retains its connection to the divine source, the Universal Mind or the All.

In their intertwined dance, the soul reaches out, consciously or unconsciously, towards the spirit for guidance and clarity. It is through this connection that moments of profound insight, inspiration, and epiphanies occur. These are the instances when the soul feels a deep resonance, a truth that transcends its earthly understanding, emanating from the spirit.

The spirit, in its eternal benevolence, constantly sends forth signals, guiding the soul towards higher truths and deeper understandings. Every intuitive nudge, every synchronicity, every dream filled with profound messages, can be seen as the spirit's way of communicating with the soul. The ancient Greek philosopher, Aristotle, once insightfully remarked,

"The soul thinks in images."

As the soul begins to attune itself more to the spirit, it starts shedding its accumulated layers, much like a snake shedding its skin. Old patterns, beliefs, and traumas that no longer serve the soul's evolution are released, making way for a clearer, purer understanding of self and existence.

This dynamic relationship is a continuous journey, a spiral towards the center, where the distinction between the soul and spirit blurs, leading to moments of unity and oneness. In these moments, the individual realizes their true nature – not just as a being having a human experience, but as a fragment of the divine, manifesting in human form. The ultimate aim of the Hermetic seeker is to achieve this state of union, where the soul is fully aligned with the spirit, experiencing the boundless love, wisdom, and bliss that such alignment brings.

Spirit and Body

The relationship between the spirit and the body is a fascinating interplay of the eternal and the transient. While the spirit is the unchanging, divine aspect of our existence, the body is our ephemeral, earthly vessel, constantly undergoing change and susceptible to the ravages of time.

The body provides the spirit with a means to experience the material world, though not in a manner where the spirit itself is changed or influenced. Instead, it's the soul that acts as the interface, processing and recording the experiences of the body, and in turn, reflecting its journey towards or away from alignment with the spirit.

Disciplines like meditation, fasting, and other spiritual practices are tools to fine-tune the body and the soul, creating an environment where the divine essence of the spirit can be more readily acknowledged and felt. The state of the body can influence the soul's ability to perceive and resonate with the spirit's guidance.

Health, vitality, and purity of the body can serve to heighten one's spiritual awareness. By maintaining a balanced and harmonious physical state, one paves the way for the soul to better attune to the spirit's eternal wisdom.

In summary, the body and spirit, while operating on different existential planes, are connected through the soul. The experiences of the body, filtered through the soul, can either bring one closer to or take one further away from recognizing the spirit's eternal and unchanging nature.

In navigating the complexities of our existence, the Hermetic tripartite model offers a lens through which we can understand our multidimensional nature. The body, our physical tether to the world, grants us the experiences and sensations of earthly life. The soul, our personal realm of emotions, memories, and thoughts, stands as the bridge—infused with our human experiences yet reaching for the divine. And the spirit, our divine spark, is our eternal and unchanging connection to the vast Universal Mind, or the All.

The intricate dance between these components is an eternal testament to the human condition, one of both mortal and immortal elements. As Plotinus wisely noted,

> Man is poised between the gods and the beasts.

It is this delicate balance that forms the essence of our journey. As we explore the depths of Hermetic teachings, we are reminded that understanding this interplay is key to our spiritual evolution, for it is by acknowledging and harmonizing these realms that we truly recognize our potential and purpose.

The Goal of Harmony

The profound Russian novelist, Fyodor Dostoevsky, opined,

> "The mystery of human existence lies not in just staying alive, but in finding something to live for."

The pursuit of harmony stands out as a paramount objective in Hermetic teachings. This isn't merely a superficial alignment but a deep, resonant attunement of the body, soul, and spirit. Each component, while unique in its nature, is intricately linked to the others, forming a cohesive whole.

The body, our tangible interface with the world, offers a plethora of experiences, sensations, and challenges. By aligning the body with the soul's aspirations and the guiding light of the spirit, one can truly harness the power and wisdom of physical existence. It's not about neglecting or denying the body but understanding its pivotal role in the spiritual journey.

The soul, our personal consciousness, is a vast repository of emotions, memories, and desires. In the Hermetic view, purifying the soul is akin to refining gold, stripping away the impurities to reveal its luminous essence. This purification is a continuous process, requiring introspection, reflection, and, most importantly, the guidance of the spirit.

Lastly, the spirit, often described as the Divine Spark, remains our constant connection to the universal consciousness or the All. It is the unchanging beacon in the ever-fluctuating journey of life. A harmonious alignment with the spirit implies not just understanding its existence but actively seeking to embody its wisdom in every facet of life.

Thus, for the Hermetic practitioner, the quest for harmony is a dynamic dance between grounding and ascension, between experiencing the earthly and yearning for the divine. This balance and harmony are not end goals but continuous processes, evolving as one delves deeper into the teachings.

As we progress through this exploration, understanding the interplay between the body, soul, and spirit becomes crucial. This foundational knowledge will set the stage for the subsequent chapters, guiding the practitioner through practical applications and deeper insights, leading them closer to unraveling the profound mysteries of existence.

The mystic poet Rumi once declared,

> "You are not a drop in the ocean. You are the entire ocean in a drop."

At the end of this chapter, I want to emphasize a few key points. If one pursues knowledge merely to feel superior, wisdom will remain elusive. It is not necessary to grasp every detail; rather, understand that we are on a journey towards something sublime, beyond the descriptive powers of material realms. Happiness and sadness, though seemingly opposite, are part of the same spectrum.

Recall the Hermetic Principle of Polarity:

> "Everything is dual; everything has poles; everything has its pair of opposites; like and unlike are the same; opposites are identical in nature, but different in degree; extremes meet; all truths are but half-truths; all paradoxes may be reconciled."

Aim to maintain balance, residing in the state of just being and observing without judgment. Avoid guilt, as it vibrates at a low frequency and can disrupt your divine alignment. Relax and recognize that you are exactly where you need to be in this evolutionary journey, or in what you might call a divine comedy.

Understanding the Spirit

The Divine Spark Within

The esteemed esoteric scholar, Manly P. Hall, once proclaimed,

> "Man is a god in the making, and as in the mystic myths of Egypt, on the potter's wheel he is being molded."

This quote underscores the inherent potential of humanity's spiritual evolution. The presence of a Divine Spark within every individual, the spirit, as understood in Hermetic philosophy, is not merely an ethereal or abstract concept but the very essence of divinity in each human being. How then does Hermeticism define and characterize this Divine Spark?

In Hermeticism, the spirit is often considered the purest form of individualized divinity. Unlike the soul, which is in a process of evolution and transformation, the spirit is immutable and eternal. It is the fragment of the ALL, the Universal Mind, that resides within each individual.

The spirit is often seen as a microcosm of the macrocosm, mirroring the qualities of the ALL or the Universal Mind. It serves as a constant link between the individual and the divine, maintaining an unbreakable connection regardless of one's physical or mental state.

In Hermeticism, the spirit is regarded as the ultimate source of wisdom, inspiration, and enlightenment. It is the inner light that guides the soul toward higher truths. When individuals access their spirit, they tap into a reservoir of divine knowledge and intuition.

While the soul engage with both spiritual and material realms, the spirit is solely focused on spiritual matters. It transcends the physical world and is unaffected by the dualities and contradictions that characterize earthly existence.

The spirit, with its innate divinity, provides a sense of purpose and destiny. It infuses the soul with the quest for higher understanding and spiritual enlightenment. This is often described as one's "higher calling" and forms the basis for spiritual evolution.

The Divine Spark, although ever-present, often lies dormant within individuals, clouded by the distractions of material life and the vagaries of the mind and emotions. Spiritual practices like meditation, prayer, and contemplative study are methods through which this divine essence can be activated or awakened.

The spirit serves as the ultimate point of unity, transcending all forms of division—whether they be physical, intellectual, or emotional. By aligning with the spirit, individuals can experience a state of oneness, not just with the divine but also with all of creation.

The spirit's role in human existence is not isolated. It works in harmony with the soul and the body to create a well-rounded human experience. While the body provides a vessel for experience and the soul navigates through these experiences for growth, the spirit acts as the divine compass guiding this intricate process. As Aristotle once declared,

> "Knowing yourself is the beginning of all wisdom."

By understanding the nature of the spirit as the Divine Spark within, one gains profound insights into the essence of human existence and the broader universe. This Divine Spark is not just a poetic notion but a crucial aspect of Hermetic teaching, serving as a beacon that guides the spiritual evolution of every individual.

Attuning the Soul to Its Divine Spark

The visionary Irish poet, William Butler Yeats, once reflected,

> "The highest we can attain to is not Knowledge, but Sympathy with Intelligence."

In Hermetic philosophy, aligning the soul with the Divine Aspect is the pinnacle of such sympathetic intelligence—a spiritual state where the individual becomes one with the higher powers that govern existence. What, then, are the methods and the meaning behind this alignment?

The first step in aligning the soul with its Divine Aspect is recognizing that such an aspect exists. In Hermetic thought, every individual holds a piece of the divine, an immutable spark that is the essence of the ALL. Acknowledging this is the foundation of alignment.

Alignment is not a passive experience but a conscious act of will and intention. It requires the harmonization of thoughts, emotions, and actions under the guidance of the spirit. Setting a clear intent to align with one's Divine Aspect helps in focusing spiritual energies toward this goal.

Meditation, prayer, and sacred rituals are traditional methods employed to facilitate alignment. These practices serve to quiet the mind, balance the emotions, and attune one's being to higher frequencies, thereby enabling better communication and union with the Divine Aspect of the spirit.

In Hermetic teachings, aligning the soul with the Divine Aspect requires a deep introspection and understanding of one's true nature. The ego, often associated with pride, desires, and attachments, can be a major impediment in this journey. Its preoccupation with the material world and transient pleasures often distracts the individual from their spiritual path. Hermeticism teaches that detachment from ego-driven desires and materialistic pursuits paves the way for aligning the soul with its Divine Aspect.

This detachment, however, shouldn't be misconstrued as a rejection of the material world. After all, it is in this very realm that we find our existence and experience the gamut of life's offerings. Instead, Hermetic wisdom advises us to see through the transience and impermanence of worldly desires, urging us to connect with the eternal and unchanging divine.

Embracing life means accepting all its shades – the joys, the sorrows, the challenges, and the victories. It's about understanding that every event, every person we meet, and every experience we undergo is part of a larger cosmic play. This understanding aids in preventing us from taking slights personally or getting overly attached to our ego-driven perceptions. By seeing the world as a divine drama, we learn the art of detachment while staying fully engaged in the dance of life. Reflecting on this perspective, Alan Watts insightfully remarked,

> "The meaning of life is just to be alive. It is so plain and so obvious and so simple. And yet, everybody rushes around in a great panic as if it were necessary to achieve something beyond themselves."

When the soul attunes itself to the spirit, its Divine Aspect, the purpose of life becomes clearer. This clarity is not just about navigating the material world but about understanding what the divine wants from you, recognizing the journey designed for you, and acknowledging the unique role you play in this vast cosmic drama. Actions and decisions are imbued with a higher sense of meaning, and the journey through the material world becomes a pathway to spiritual enlightenment.

To align with the Divine Aspect is transformative. By understanding who you are at your core, your authentic self, you begin to grasp the part you play in the grand scheme of things. Embracing both the joys and sorrows of life, you find yourself moving fluidly with the universe's will. It not only enriches spiritual understanding but also has tangible impacts on mental, emotional, and even physical well-being. This alignment, when nurtured, can lead to healing, better relationships, and an enhanced sense of peace and contentment.

Alignment is not a one-time event but a continuous process. The influences of the material world, changes in personal circumstances, and the complexities of human emotions require that the alignment be maintained and adjusted over time. Resisting the predetermined role or path causes friction; embracing it brings harmony. The key is to accept, with grace, the script of the divine drama, playing your role with dedication and authenticity.

Once aligned, individuals often experience synchronicities—meaningful coincidences that serve as indicators of spiritual harmony. These are not mere chance events but signs that one is truly operating in sync with the greater universal energies, indicating that they are flowing in tandem with the will of the universe.

By earnestly practicing these methods and cultivating an awareness of the Divine Aspect, one can align their soul with this higher reality. This alignment is a sublime state, bridging the gap between the material and the spiritual, the finite and the infinite. It offers not just enlightenment but a way of being, an elevated existence where every action, thought, and emotion is an expression of the divine within.

Understanding this role, discerning the divine will, and aligning oneself with it is the key. It means embracing life in all its facets – the joys, the sorrows, the challenges, and the triumphs. Rather than seeing life's experiences as random or chaotic, it's about viewing them as part of a grander design, orchestrated by the universe or the Divine Aspect.

As individuals, the task then becomes to transcend the ego, to not take the events of life personally or be ensnared by them. Instead, we should aim to flow with the universe's will, accepting the role we are destined to play and executing it with grace and wisdom. This doesn't mean a passive acceptance of fate but an active engagement with life, fueled by a deep understanding of one's authentic self and divine purpose.

In doing so, the soul starts to resonate with the Divine Aspect. The cacophony of ego-driven desires subsides, and in its place, there's a harmonious symphony, a dance of the soul with the rhythms of the universe. The alignment becomes a continuous journey, a dynamic process where the soul learns, grows, and evolves, drawing ever closer to the divine essence from which it originated. The British philosopher, Alan Watts, insightfully remarked,

> "The only way to make sense out of change is to plunge into it, move with it, and join the dance."

Yet, to truly grasp this harmonious dance, one must also fathom the underpinning principle behind it: The Principle of Vibration which states,

"Nothing rests; everything moves; everything vibrates."

This principle emphasizes that every atom, every facet of our being, every intangible thought, and even the very soul itself is in a state of constant motion and vibration. When one recognizes this ceaseless movement and inherent rhythm, attuning to the Divine becomes more than just a concept—it becomes a visceral, tangible experience. Just as a musician attunes an instrument to produce harmony, so too can we attune our soul's vibration to that of the Divine.

Remember and understand, life is not a chaotic dance but a harmonious rhythm. When we align our soul with the divine spark within and recognize the omnipresent vibrations around and within us, every step, every thought, every moment becomes a divine expression.

At the end of this chapter, let us reflect on a few profound ideas. We are manifestations who are bound, yet the ultimate reality is unbounded, without beginning, middle, or end. This absolute reality resides in the hearts of all creatures; it is the beginning, the middle, and the end of all beings. It encompasses the mind, the consciousness of creatures, the God of gods. It is fire and mountain, genderless, water, ocean, the single syllable, the wind, the crocodile, the undecaying time, death, and the source of what is yet to come. It is the dice in the gamblers' hands, the brilliance of the lustrous, the victory and bravery of the courageous, the seed of all beings. Without it, nothing can exist, animate or inanimate. It supports the entire universe with merely a fragment of itself.

Yet, what does this vast knowledge mean to you if you do not realize that it also resides within you?

Be passionate and compassionate towards yourself and others.

The Alchemy of Existence

Mind's Dance with Spirit, Soul, and Body

In the profound depths of Hermetic understanding, the interplay between the mind, spirit, soul, and body unveils a mesmerizing dance of interconnectedness. The soul, timeless in its existence, remains not as an unyielding constant but as a vessel of ceaseless evolution and learning within the material world. As we delve into this dance, we'll explore how the mind becomes the stage upon which the soul, influenced by the guiding light of the spirit, interacts with the tangible realm of the body. Together, these elements shape our experiences, our perceptions, and ultimately, our journey towards higher understanding.

The soul's journey is a paradox. It is, by nature, timeless and unchanging. Yet, its passage through the physical world is marked by experiences, lessons, growth, and a constant striving towards higher truths. It's akin to a diamond that, though eternally brilliant, still goes through processes of refinement to reveal its truest shine.

Enter the spirit, the divine spark within. While the soul embarks on its educational sojourn, the spirit stands as its guide, its North Star, guiding it towards alignment with the divine order. The spirit, in its purest essence, remains untainted and serves as a constant reminder of the soul's origins and ultimate purpose.

Now, where does the mind fit into this profound dynamic? The mind acts as the interface, the medium through which the soul navigates the complexities of the material world. Through the mind, the soul perceives, learns, feels, and engages. It's the tool the soul uses to interpret, understand, and interact with the physical realm. The mind, thus, becomes the playground where experiences are felt, lessons are learned, and wisdom is gained. It's through the mind that the soul finds its expression, gives voice to its desires, and confronts its challenges.

However, it's crucial to understand that while the mind serves the soul, it is not always in perfect harmony with the spirit's divine guidance. The challenges, distractions, and lures of the physical realm can sometimes mislead the mind, causing detours in the soul's journey. When the individual consciousness (the mind) aligns with the universal consciousness (the spirit), the soul finds its true path, harmoniously blending its eternal nature with its worldly experiences.

The soul, within the Hermetic worldview, is often seen as the bridge between the ethereal and the tangible. It's the eternal traveler, journeying across realms and lifetimes, bearing the essence of consciousness. To quote the Corpus Hermeticum:

> "The soul is immortal, and it has the power of eternal thought."

This unchanging, undying nature of the soul establishes it as a being beyond the physical realm.

However, the paradox arises when we consider the soul's continuous evolution. While its ultimate essence is divine light, and this core remains unchanged, its experiences, knowledge, and wisdom continuously expand. Every journey, every challenge, and every joy adds to its fabric of understanding. But from where does the soul derive these experiences?

Enter the body and the mind. If the soul is the eternal traveler, the body is its temporary vessel, and the mind is its compass. The body, bound by the physical realm, provides the soul with a means to interact with the world—a tangible presence in an otherwise intangible existence. It's through the body that the soul can touch, taste, hear, see, and feel the wonders of the earthly plane.

The mind, on the other hand, is a more intricate vehicle. It's the domain of thought, emotion, and imagination. While the body perceives the external world, the mind interprets it. Every sensory input, every emotion, every perception is processed through this remarkable instrument. As Hermes Trismegistus once stated,

> "The mind is the key to understanding."

Moreover, the mind holds the potential for both our greatest achievements and our deepest pitfalls. It's where dreams are birthed and where fears take root. It's where the soul contemplates its existence, reflects upon its experiences, and seeks alignment with its divine purpose.

In conclusion, while the soul remains the eternal beacon of our existence, anchored and guided by the spirit—the divine spark within—it relies heavily on the mind and body as its indispensable partners in the grand journey of existence. Through their harmonious collaboration, the soul not only finds expression and experiences the richness of life, but it also aligns more closely with its spiritual essence, progressing in its eternal quest for understanding and evolution.

Interplay of the Eternal Soul and the Evolving Mind

In the intricate landscape of Hermetic philosophy, the interplay between the soul and the mind unfolds with profound significance. Each holds a unique position, but together, they craft a cohesive narrative that illuminates our understanding of existence, purpose, and spiritual evolution. The Hermetic text, the Kybalion, profoundly states,

> "The lips of wisdom are closed, except to the ears of Understanding."

Hinting at the profound interconnection between the mind's intellectual prowess and the soul's intrinsic wisdom. Our mind, a masterful instrument, equips the soul with tools such as logic, emotion, and imagination. These enable the soul—a beacon of eternal consciousness and identity—to navigate, interpret, and interact with the multifaceted fabric of life.

The mind, while deeply rooted in the temporal and earthly, serves as the soul's bridge to the material realm. It's through this conduit that the soul gathers experiences, imbibes lessons, and continually refines its understanding. For while the soul stands as an immutable pillar of light, its purpose within the material realm is, paradoxically, evolution and growth. The wisdom of ancient Greece echoes through time with the profound adage,

"Man, know thyself."

This call for introspection and self-awareness was not just a philosophical musing but a foundational tenet for a meaningful life.

The mind serves as the intellectual and rational apparatus through which the soul navigates and interprets the world. While the soul is the essence of individual consciousness and identity, the mind provides the tools—logic, emotion, imagination—for the soul to engage with its environment.

In Hermeticism, the soul represents the inner, eternal, and unchanging reality, whereas the mind is more aligned with temporal, earthly experiences. The mind is the mechanism that allows the soul to interact with the material world, making it possible for the soul to gather experiences, learn lessons, and evolve.

While the mind accumulates knowledge through sensory experience and intellectual pursuit, the soul harbors wisdom, which is an understanding that transcends earthly limitations. Wisdom is considered the higher octave of knowledge and serves as the guiding force for the mind.

In sum, by delving deep into the intricate relationship between the soul and the mind, we unlock portals of understanding that illuminate the very essence of human consciousness and our spiritual trajectory. Hermetic philosophy doesn't view them as mere isolated entities but as intertwined aspects of a grander whole. Together, they chart the course of our life's voyage, navigating the challenges, joys, and mysteries of our existential journey.

As we conclude this chapter, let's take a moment to reflect deeply on the inner workings of our minds. Observe the thoughts arising within you and consider the shadowy aspects of your psyche that are clamoring for light and acceptance. When you reside in the present, free from judgment and guilt, you connect with the universal mind where the magic unfolds. The key to this connection lies in acting without attachment to outcomes and with heartfelt compassion.

Embrace the dynamic interplay of fire and earth: let the fiery spirit of initiative ignite your actions, while grounded wisdom stabilizes your journey. By aligning your actions with a blend of bravery and prudence, you invite the universe to co-create a reality brimming with achievement and fulfillment. Trust in your path, engage fully with your spirit, and observe as the world aligns to support your ascent. This is the essence of living authentically and abundantly, where each step in true alignment draws you closer to the divine dance of creation.

"Get Out of Your Own Way." Float on the breeze of positive thoughts, allowing your trust in yourself to be the wind beneath your wings. Imagine planting seeds of belief deep within the soil of your soul, nurturing them with the conviction that the universe is conspiring to assist you. Envision being enveloped in a warm, invisible cloak that assures you are exactly where you need to be, safe and secure.

Let us cherish the melody of living authentically, honoring every strength and weakness. Floating on the breeze of positive thoughts, let's plant our dreams with intention and then, with spirits liberated from our own confines, step back. The universe is not merely crafting our journey; it invites us to co-create at every twist and turn.

The Principle of Mentalism

"The All is Mind; The Universe is Mental"

The Hermetic philosophy draws upon a set of principles that form the bedrock of its teachings. One such principle is succinctly captured by the statement,

> "The All is Mind; The Universe is Mental."

This Principle of Mentalism postulates that everything we observe, experience, or even that which remains beyond our direct perception is an emanation of a singular, omnipotent Mind.

This Universal Mind, often referred to as 'The All', isn't just a remote entity observing the cosmos from a distance. Instead, it's intimately entwined with every particle, every thought, and every occurrence. To say that the Universe is mental is to recognize that the foundational substance of reality is not matter or energy, but consciousness itself. This consciousness isn't just passive; it's active, intentional, and purposeful.

Parallel to this is the axiom from the Emerald Tablet:

> "As above, so below; as within, so without."

This is the Principle of Correspondence. It proposes that there is a mirrored correspondence between all levels of reality. What happens on a macrocosmic scale has its reflection on a microcosmic scale, and vice versa. The patterns and laws observed in the vastness of the cosmos can also be seen at play in the minutiae of individual existence.

Connecting these two principles, one begins to see a network of interconnected thought. If the Universal Mind is the fabric from which all reality springs, then the Principle of Correspondence is the pattern upon that fabric, ensuring that every thread is in its rightful place, reflecting the greater design. Together, these ideas suggest that understanding one's own mind and inner world can offer insights into the wider universe, and that by aligning with this Universal Mind, one can attain greater harmony and wisdom.

In Hermetic philosophy, 'The All' is the absolute, the originator of all that exists. It is an incomprehensible and undefinable entity that is beyond our material understanding. While we may not grasp its full nature, we can comprehend its expression through the mental substance that manifests as the universe.

"The All is Mind; The Universe is Mental."

According to this principle, the entire cosmos is a construct of the Universal Mind. Every physical object, every event, and every being is a manifestation of this mental energy. It's not a matter of the mind creating a separate, external reality but rather that reality itself is intrinsically mental.

What does this mean for our understanding of existence? The Principle of Mentalism posits that the material world isn't an isolated, arbitrary realm. Instead, it is the physical expression of the spiritual or mental realm. This understanding transforms our perspective on the universe. Instead of seeing the spiritual and material as two separate domains, the Hermeticist recognizes them as two sides of the same coin, both emanating from the singular Universal Mind.

In practical terms, this principle highlights the transformative power of thought and intention. If all is mind, then our individual and collective thoughts, beliefs, and intentions play a crucial role in shaping our experiences and reality. It underscores the inherent connectedness of everything and everyone, suggesting that the inner workings of our mind are, in many ways, a reflection of the grander universe outside. By understanding and harnessing this principle, one can potentially influence their personal reality and, by extension, the greater world around them.

In the intricate framework of Hermetic philosophy, the notion of the mind assumes a central, pivotal role. At the very core of this idea is the Universal Mind—often referred to as 'The All'. This isn't merely a grandiose version of human thought processes or cognition. Instead, the Universal Mind is both the source and the manifestation, an omnipresent consciousness from which everything in existence springs forth.

The Universal Mind is the infinite, omnipresent consciousness from which all things emanate. It's not simply a grander version of human consciousness; it is the primordial, undifferentiated source of all existence. Every manifestation in the universe, is an expression or projection of this Universal Mind. It is both the creator and the creation, maintaining a singular, cohesive intelligence that underpins and permeates everything.

In parallel to this overarching Universal Mind is the individual mind. While perceived as an autonomous entity, it is not a direct fragment of the Universal Mind but rather a fragment of its emanation. Think of it as a droplet of water in the vast ocean; while it holds its own distinct position, it carries the essence and properties of the ocean from which it originates. This droplet metaphor encapsulates the essence of our consciousness, where each thought, emotion, or perception is imbued with a hint of the cosmic.

However, the waters can sometimes be turbulent. Our personal emotions, thoughts, perceptions, even the negative ones, arise from a multitude of factors — our environment, our experiences, and our soul's journey. The appearance of negative emotions doesn't necessarily stem directly from the Universal Mind, but rather the misalignment or discord between our individual soul and the spirit — the divine spark within us. The more misaligned we are, the more likely we are to perceive and interpret events through a skewed, shadowed lens, leading to these negative states of consciousness. The Hermetic principle,

"As above, so below; as within, so without"

provides insight into this. Our external experiences often mirror our internal state of being. When the soul is not aligned with the spirit, the result can be negative emotions or turmoil within, which then manifests externally in our life experiences. Conversely, when there's alignment and harmony between the soul and spirit, the individual experiences peace, clarity, and positive emotions.

In essence, the outer world becomes a reflection of one's inner world. The journey, then, is about realigning, recalibrating, and harmonizing the soul with the spirit to create balance, both internally and externally. Through this alignment, the individual can begin to channel the Universal Mind's vast cosmic consciousness more clearly and effectively, bringing about a state of equilibrium and heightened understanding.

Since the universe is a mental construct, thoughts hold incredible power. In Hermetic practices, mental disciplines like visualization, affirmation, and meditation are used to manifest desires and bring about change. The power of thought is not just a psychological tool but a metaphysical principle that can shape reality.

Understanding the Principle of Mentalism has profound spiritual implications. It helps one grasp the unity of all existence and the divine nature of consciousness. This understanding enables individuals to align their actions, thoughts, and emotions with higher spiritual truths.

When one fully grasps and internalizes the Principle of Mentalism, a state of 'cosmic consciousness' may be achieved. This is a heightened state of awareness where the individual feels at one with the Universal Mind, comprehending the interconnectedness of all things.

The Principle of Mentalism is not just a theoretical concept but has practical applications in daily life. Understanding that "The All is Mind; The Universe is Mental" empowers individuals to take control of their thoughts, thereby influencing their reality in both subtle and significant ways.

By fully understanding and applying the Principle of Mentalism, one can unlock a transformative way of engaging with the world. It offers a unique lens through which to view reality, emphasizing the power and primacy of the mind in shaping our experiences and understanding the mysteries of existence.

Practical Applications

The visionary thinker, Bob Proctor, confidently asserts,

"Thoughts become things. If you see it in your mind, you will hold it in your hand."

This statement takes a fresh yet timeless perspective on the Hermetic Principle of Mentalism, which states, "The All is Mind; The Universe is Mental." But how can we put this ancient wisdom to practical use in our modern lives? Let's delve into the practical applications.

Thought Management for Manifestation

In Hermetic teachings, the concept that "The All is Mind; The Universe is Mental" holds a pivotal place. This notion suggests that the vast expanse of the cosmos is a direct emanation or projection of the Universal Mind—a boundless, omnipresent consciousness. When one truly grasps this profound idea, it has profound implications for our understanding of personal empowerment and creation.

From the vast cosmic scale of the Universal Mind, we zoom into the microcosm of our individual minds. Just as the universe is an expression of the Universal Mind, our personal realities are a manifestation of our individual minds. This gives credence to the idea that our thoughts, beliefs, and intentions have tangible power over the fabric of our lived experiences. The saying, "As within, so without" from the Hermetic Emerald Tablet can be seen as a direct reflection of this principle. It suggests that our internal mental state, our beliefs, emotions, and intentions, directly influence and shape our external reality.

Now, let's consider techniques such as positive affirmations, visualization, and focused intention. These aren't merely psychological strategies for boosting confidence or motivation; they are, in the Hermetic view, powerful tools that tap into the inherent ability of our minds to shape and mold our reality. Positive affirmations, when repeated with genuine belief and emotion, serve to reshape our internal landscape, replacing limiting beliefs with empowering ones. Over time, this transformed internal state begins to project outwardly, attracting circumstances that align with our affirmed beliefs.

Visualization is another potent tool. By creating a vivid mental picture of a desired outcome, emotion, or scenario, we are essentially providing a 'blueprint' for our reality. The Hermetic axiom, "As above, so below," reinforces this idea. By visualizing or imagining (the "above" or mental plane), we begin the process of bringing that vision into physical manifestation (the "below" or material plane).

Focused intention takes this a step further. It's not just about holding a thought or a vision, but directing our energy, will, and desire towards a specific outcome. It's a concentrated effort, a sharpened mental directive aimed at manifesting a particular result.

From the foundational texts of Hermetic wisdom, the Corpus Hermeticum, comes a profound insight into the interplay between thought and understanding:

"For the mind, thinking of itself, speaks or says the word; but it is the reason which hears, being present with the mind."

This emphasizes the active role of the mind in creation, and how intention (reason) works in tandem with thought.

In essence, when we understand and embrace the Hermetic principles, tools like affirmations, visualization, and intention become more than mere techniques—they are keys that unlock the transformative power of the mind, allowing us to co-create our reality in harmony with the greater Universal Mind.

Emotional Intelligence and Mindfulness

Emotional intelligence and mindfulness, in the light of the Principle of Mentalism, offer us valuable tools for navigating our complex inner landscapes. This principle suggests that the mind is foundational to all of reality; hence, understanding and mastering our own mental and emotional states become paramount in our journey through life.

At the core of emotional intelligence lies the ability to recognize, understand, and manage our emotions. This involves acknowledging the full spectrum of our feelings, both positive and negative, without pushing them away or becoming overwhelmed. As the stoic philosopher Marcus Aurelius once stated,

> "You have power over your mind – not outside events. Realize this, and you will find strength."

This understanding emphasizes the importance of personal agency in how we respond to our emotions.

Mindfulness complements emotional intelligence by training us to be present with our feelings without judgment. Instead of avoiding or suppressing negative emotions, mindfulness encourages us to sit with them, observe them, and let them pass naturally. As Thich Nhat Hanh wisely said,

> "Feelings come and go like clouds in a windy sky. Conscious breathing is my anchor."

Through consistent mindfulness practice, one can learn that negative emotions, no matter how intense, are transient and have no lasting power over us.

Every day, and even every hour, our minds are inundated with numerous thoughts and emotions. The task is not to cling to or push them away, but simply to experience them, understanding their fleeting nature. However, the choice of which emotion to act upon, lies within our realm of control. It's like being at the helm of a ship amidst a stormy sea; while we cannot control the waves and the wind, we can adjust our sails and steer our ship in the direction we desire.

This understanding can be further enriched by considering the Hermetic principle of Rhythm, which states,

"Everything flows, out and in; everything has its tides; all things rise and fall."

Just as a pendulum swings to the left and then to the right, in rhythm, our thoughts and emotions have their ebb and flow. By recognizing this natural rhythm, we can better navigate our mental states, and instead of being swept away by the highs and lows, we can find balance, just as a pendulum eventually finds its center.

In conclusion, as Rumi poetically expressed,

"This being human is a guest house. Every morning a new arrival."

Remind us that emotions, like these temporary guests, are fleeting. Thus, the mastery of our mental realm and the discernment to know which emotions to act upon is truly in our hands. By embracing all facets of our emotional experiences and using the tools of emotional intelligence and mindfulness, we can find deeper understanding, resilience, and wisdom in our journey through life.

Decision Making and Problem Solving

Decision-making and problem-solving are fundamental aspects of our lives, and the realization that our thoughts have the power to shape reality brings a transformative perspective to these processes.

At the heart of this realization is the idea that we are not merely passive actors reacting to challenges but active creators with the ability to shape our circumstances. This sentiment echoes the words of George Bernard Shaw, who remarked,

"Life isn't about finding yourself. Life is about creating yourself."

Rather than waiting for problems to arise and then tackling them, we can take charge and mold circumstances to our advantage.

This proactive mindset changes the dynamics of how we approach challenges. It means that instead of perpetually being in a state of 'putting out fires,' we are 'fireproofing' our environment. It encourages forward-thinking and foresight. As Wayne Dyer aptly put it,

> "Change the way you look at things, and the things you look at change."

By aligning our thoughts and actions with our desired outcomes, we can shift from merely reacting to challenges to actively shaping our reality.

Furthermore, when problems do arise, this mindset equips us with a sense of empowerment. As Albert Einstein famously said,

> "We cannot solve our problems with the same thinking we used when we created them."

With the understanding that our thoughts are potent tools, we can approach issues with creativity and innovation.

In essence, realizing the power of our thoughts in decision-making and problem-solving illuminates the proactive potential we hold. It reminds us of the wisdom in the words of Mahatma Gandhi,

> "You must be the change you want to see in the world."

By consciously shaping our thoughts, we can not only navigate challenges but also create a reality where challenges are fewer and far between. Yet, to truly master this art of shaping reality, it's imperative we recognize and harmonize the dual energies within us, as highlighted in the core teachings of Hermeticism.

In the realm of Hermeticism, the Principle of Gender resonates deeply, emphasizing that,

> "Gender is in everything; everything has its masculine and feminine principles."

This notion transcends mere biological distinctions; it speaks to the inherent energies and qualities present in all things.

When applied to decision-making and problem-solving, this principle suggests that a holistic approach—one that harnesses both masculine and feminine energies—can be most effective. The masculine energy can be seen as assertive, logical, and analytical, driving toward solutions with precision and clarity. On the other hand, the feminine energy embodies intuition, compassion, and creativity, offering a broader perspective and fostering collaboration.

By harmoniously blending these energies in our problem-solving endeavors, we ensure a more comprehensive, balanced, and dynamic approach. This union of energies allows for solutions that are not only effective but also well-rounded and adaptable to varying circumstances.

In conclusion, just as the Hermetic Principle of Gender speaks of the intrinsic duality in all things, our approach to challenges should embrace both the masculine and feminine. Recognizing and harnessing these energies can enrich our decision-making processes and lead us to solutions that resonate with the intricate dance of life itself.

Health and Well-being

Health and well-being are intricately tied to our mental states, and the Principle of Mentalism offers profound insights into the depth of this connection. The mind doesn't merely influence the body; it shapes its health, vitality, and even its capacity for healing.

The notion that "your body is a vessel for your soul" is emblematic of the intertwined relationship between the physical and the mental. A healthy vessel not only sustains but can enhance the soul's experiences. Consequently, investing in a healthy lifestyle—be it through nutrition, exercise, or rest—is not just a matter of physical sustenance but also of spiritual enrichment. As the Romans would put it,

> "A sound mind in a sound body."

In addition to the tangible aspects of health, the tools and techniques rooted in Hermetic principles further emphasize the depth of the mind-body connection. Guided imagery and meditation, for instance, are not just exercises in relaxation. They harness the mind's potential to shape reality, including the reality of one's own body. As Buddha once declared,

> "What you think, you become."

Positive affirmations, too, play a pivotal role. They are not just idle words; they are declarations of intent, signals to both the conscious and subconscious mind to manifest the desired state of health. As Louise Hay, known for her teachings on affirmations and positive thinking, stated,

> "Every thought we think is creating our future."

In embracing the Principle of Mentalism, we are also acknowledging the immense power that our mental state holds over our physical health. The proactive nurturing of positive, health-affirming thoughts and practices becomes more than self-care; it's an act of self-love and self-preservation. To quote Hippocrates, often regarded as the father of medicine,

> "Natural forces within us are the true healers of disease."

Thus, understanding and embracing the profound relationship between mind and body is not just beneficial but vital for holistic well-being.

The Ongoing Journey of Mastery

Mastering the practical applications of the Principle of Mentalism is a lifelong journey. It requires continuous practice, learning, and refinement. But as you grow more proficient in applying this principle, you'll find that the boundary between the mental and the physical becomes increasingly porous, and the possibilities for manifesting your desired reality become endless.

By understanding and integrating the practical implications of the Principle of Mentalism, individuals can lead a life marked by empowerment, clarity, and a deepened connection with the universal energies that guide our existence. It's not just a philosophical principle but a tangible, applicable law that has the power to transform every aspect of human life. To truly ascend on this journey of mastery, one must grapple with the Hermetic Principle of Polarity.

"Everything is dual; everything has poles; everything has its pair of opposites."

In our material realm, we often see the world through the lens of dichotomies—good and evil, light and dark, knowledge and ignorance. Yet, these are but different poles of the same spectrum. Their differences are not of kind, but of degree.

All truths are but half-truths, and every truth inevitably carries its shadow of falsehood. Heat and cold, for instance, are not distinct entities but are of the same nature. Their perceived opposition comes merely from the varying degrees between them. Opposites can indeed be reconciled when we grasp their inherent interconnectedness.

To harness the transformative power of the mind, we must think beyond these dichotomies. By recognizing the continuum between opposites, we unlock a more profound understanding and control of our mental faculties. Mastery is not merely about choosing one pole over the other, but harmonizing and navigating the degrees between them.

In essence, seeing beyond the apparent duality and embracing the truth that opposites are unified at their core brings us closer to the mastery of our reality.

Reincarnation

What is Reincarnation?

Reincarnation, within the Hermetic framework, transcends mere sequential lives, becoming a profound avenue for the soul's evolution. It is not just a cyclical return to the material realm but a nuanced journey of the soul, inching ever closer to divinity with each sojourn.

At the core of this understanding is the belief that the soul is an undying entity, poised with potentialities that it unfurls with every incarnation. Each earthly life serves as a schoolroom, offering a plethora of experiences, challenges, joys, and sorrows. The soul learns, grows, and undergoes a metamorphosis of sorts with each lifetime, collecting wisdom and inching closer to its divine essence.

Hermetic teachings assert that man is not a passive participant in the grand design of existence. Instead, he possesses an active agency, holding the power to understand the universe's workings and, in that profound understanding, even touching the very essence of the divine. Timothy Freke, delving deep into the heart of Hermetic thought, asserts,

> "The Hermetic philosophy places man at the very centre of God's creation. Hermes declares that 'man is a marvel'. With his mind he may not only understand the universe, but even come to know God. He is not a mortal body which will live and die. He is an immortal soul which, through the experience of a spiritual rebirth, may become a god."

This knowledge isn't limited to cosmic mechanics but extends to a deep, personal communion with the Divine.

Yet, the journey towards such enlightenment isn't a linear path nor a singular lifetime's endeavor. It is iterative and expansive. Just as gold is repeatedly melted to rid it of impurities, the soul undergoes numerous incarnations to shed its illusions and ascend in its wisdom. Each life is a chapter, a distinct story, with its unique lessons, building upon the narrative of the soul's eternal saga.

The assertion that man is not "a mortal body which will live and die" but an "immortal soul which, through the experience of a spiritual rebirth, may become a god" captures the grand vision Hermeticism has for humanity. This spiritual rebirth isn't confined to a singular event but is experienced across countless lifetimes, with the soul refining its essence, understanding its true nature, and moving closer to the Divine.

In essence, reincarnation in Hermetic philosophy isn't just about rebirth in a physical sense, but the continuous rebirthing of the soul as it spirals upwards in its divine ascent, shedding the transient and embracing the eternal.

The Cycle of Souls

Hermetic philosophy introduces us to a notion that's both intriguing and comforting: the journey of the soul is not confined to a singular lifetime but threads through a continuous fabric of existence known as 'The Cycle of Souls.' This cycle, like the revolutions of a wheel, suggests movement, progression, and renewal.

Reincarnation in Hermetic thought isn't merely about rebirth in a new physical form, but it's a crucial facet of the soul's mission: the quest for enlightenment and unity with the Universal Mind or the 'All.' This journey, while undeniably vast, is not endless. The objective isn't just to live myriad lives but to extract wisdom, understanding, and growth from each incarnation.

Each terrestrial journey offers the soul a fresh canvas – a chance to confront different challenges, embrace varied joys, and navigate through distinct sorrows. These experiences, no matter how contrasting, cumulatively propel the soul closer to its ultimate purpose: to realize and embrace its inherent divinity.

So, every time the soul engages in the physical realm, it's akin to a student entering a new grade in school, equipped with lessons from the previous year, ready for new teachings, and aiming for graduation. The environments may differ, the lessons might vary in complexity, but the educational trajectory aims towards a holistic understanding and eventual graduation.

In the end, the "Cycle of Souls" represents the soul's evolutionary pathway. It is the grand journey of return, of rediscovering its origin and reuniting with the infinite expanse of the Universal Mind. Through this cyclical process, the soul isn't aimlessly wandering but purposefully advancing, aligning more with its source after each incarnation.

Karma and Reincarnation

Karma, a term often associated with Eastern philosophies, finds resonance in Hermetic teachings, albeit without the explicit label. At its core, karma represents the universal law of cause and effect, a doctrine suggesting that every action generates a corresponding response. In Hermeticism, this principle is beautifully encapsulated in the idea that nothing occurs in isolation; everything is interconnected, bound by the cosmic rhythm of action and reaction. The ancient Hermetic adage proclaims,

"Every cause has its effect; every effect has its cause."

One's actions, whether physical, emotional, or mental, emanate ripples throughout the vast fabric of existence. These energetic imprints, akin to seeds sown in the fertile ground of the universe, eventually bear fruit. Often, the consequences of these actions aren't immediately realized but may manifest in subsequent lifetimes, contributing to the circumstances, challenges, and blessings of those incarnations.

This interplay between action and consequence, cause and effect, shapes the trajectory of the soul's journey through the cycle of reincarnation. Each life, thus, becomes a chapter in a larger narrative, where the soul grapples with unresolved issues, redeems past actions, and strives for spiritual growth and alignment. The choices made, lessons learned, and debts repaid in one lifetime influence the circumstances of the next. In this way, the soul is both the author and the protagonist of its intricate story of evolution.

The idea of karma within the Hermetic framework serves as a potent reminder of the profound responsibility each individual holds. Every thought entertained, emotion felt, and action taken has implications, not just for the immediate surroundings or the present life, but for the broader cosmic balance and the soul's continued journey through reincarnation. It underscores the importance of living with intention, consciousness, and moral integrity, knowing that the echoes of our choices reverberate through time and space.

In this interwoven fabric of cause and effect, every soul has an opportunity for redemption, learning, and growth. The idea of karma within the Hermetic framework is not merely about retribution; it's about understanding and embracing the profound responsibility we hold in the grand scheme of things. Every choice we make, every action we commit, sends ripples throughout the vast cosmos, influencing not just our current existence but the trajectories of our future lives. It serves as a potent reminder to tread the path of life with intention, awareness, and a deep respect for the interconnectedness of all things.

The Veil of Forgetfulness

Within the grand mosaic of Hermetic reincarnation, there's a prevailing mystery: Why don't we retain clear memories of our past lives? This enigma is often ascribed to the 'Veil of Forgetfulness,' a metaphorical shroud that dims our consciousness to past incarnations as we enter a new life.

While each incarnation offers the soul a fresh slate, allowing it to experience, grow, and evolve without the overt biases and burdens of previous lives, it's not devoid of influence from the past. This subtle influence is where the concept of karma intertwines with the Veil of Forgetfulness. Even as the veil ensures our conscious mind starts afresh, the imprints of our past actions – our karma – persist at a deeper, soulful level.

Karma, in this context, serve as a guiding force. It subtly directs our soul's journey, ensuring that the lessons needing learning, the experiences required for our evolution, find their way to us. If we were to constantly recall past mistakes, regrets, or even successes, our current journey might become overshadowed, preventing us from embracing the lessons of the present. Yet, our karmic imprints ensure that while the explicit memories fade, the essence of our experiences and the wisdom derived from them remain.

This duality – of forgetting explicit memories while retaining the essence of past experiences – is what makes the reincarnative journey so profound. Unexplainable fears, instincts, déjà vu, or affinities towards certain cultures or epochs might very well be our soul's way of hinting at our past, moments where the veil becomes slightly translucent.

In essence, the Veil of Forgetfulness, when seen alongside karma, is a compassionate design. It allows each life to be a distinct chapter, free from explicit past entanglements, but always subtly influenced by the wisdom and lessons the soul has amassed over eons.

The Purpose and Process

The renowned esoteric philosopher, Manly P. Hall, poignantly remarked,

"Death is but a doorway to new dimensions of life."

This sentiment echoes a core aspect of Hermetic philosophy, which sees death not as an end, but rather as a transition in the soul's eternal journey. While the concept of reincarnation is addressed in various philosophical and religious frameworks, Hermetic philosophy offers a unique lens through which to understand the purpose and process behind this phenomenon.

The ultimate purpose behind the cycle of reincarnation in Hermetic thought is the evolution of the soul. But what does evolution mean in this context? It refers to the soul's journey towards achieving higher states of consciousness, wisdom, and ultimately, union with the Universal Mind or the 'All.' Every life is a set of lessons, a playground for growth, where the soul learns to navigate complexities, challenges, and opportunities.

Imagine each life as a grade level in the school of spiritual growth. You enroll in various 'courses,' so to speak—like Relationships 101, Ethical Conduct, or Emotional Mastery—that are suited to your soul's specific needs and areas for development. The 'exams' are the real-world challenges that test your understanding and application of these spiritual and moral lessons. Failure is not a setback but a stepping stone for growth, as the soul will continue to face similar challenges in subsequent lives until the lesson is fully absorbed.

In Hermetic philosophy, the actions, thoughts, and intentions of each life contribute to what could be termed a 'karmic ledger.' This is an energetic account of the soul's deeds and experiences. Positive actions may yield 'karmic credit,' making it easier for the soul to attain higher states of consciousness in future lives. Conversely, negative actions accumulate as 'karmic debt,' which the soul will need to 'repay' through future challenges and trials.

Hermeticism often depicts the reincarnation cycle as less linear than some Eastern philosophies do. You're not necessarily moving in a straight line from 'lower' to 'higher' states but might engage in a more complex, web-like journey that offers diverse experiences beneficial for your soul's evolution.

Between Lives: The Astral Plane

Hermetic teachings propose that after physical death, the soul enters an astral plane or a spiritual realm where it reviews the lessons learned in the previous life and prepares for the next incarnation. This phase is not eternal; it serves as a transitional period where the soul reorients itself for the next leg of its evolutionary journey.

Traditional notions of heaven and hell, as fixed destinations of reward or punishment, are seen differently through the Hermetic lens. Instead of viewing them as distinct places, they can be understood more as states of being or consciousness. As the philosopher Thomas Hobbes aptly remarked,

"Hell is truth seen too late."

This might be interpreted in a Hermetic context as the realization of one's ignorance or missed opportunities after departing the physical realm.

On the other hand, the so-called 'heaven' could be seen as achieving a state of enlightenment, a profound alignment with the Universal Mind. As Oliver Goldsmith observed,

> "Life is a journey that must be traveled no matter how bad the roads and accommodations."

Implying that our experiences, whether challenging or rewarding, serve a purpose in our spiritual evolution.

Rainer Maria Rilke's words,

> "The only journey is the one within."

Further encapsulate the Hermetic view, suggesting that our true spiritual progression lies in the inward exploration of the self, understanding our actions, intentions, and their consequences.

So what happens when the soul completes its curriculum? In Hermeticism, it is believed that once the soul has reached a certain level of wisdom and enlightenment, it may opt out of the cycle of reincarnation, achieving a permanent union with the Universal Mind. This is the end goal of the soul's journey—a state of ultimate enlightenment, where the soul returns to its source and becomes one with the All.

One of the most empowering aspects of the Hermetic view of reincarnation is the concept of personal agency. Through conscious efforts like meditation, ethical living, and spiritual practice, individuals can influence the trajectory of their soul's journey.

Understanding the purpose and process of reincarnation in Hermetic philosophy can significantly enrich your perception of life, death, and what lies beyond. It offers a roadmap for the soul's journey, illuminating the path towards higher wisdom, deeper understanding, and ultimate union with the Universal Mind.

As we conclude this chapter, let's reflect on a few key ideas. The concept of Karma, fundamentally linked to action, poses a question: does it mean we should refrain from taking action and emulate Buddha? Remember, that was Buddha's path—his dharma and karma. For you, the call is to act without fixating on the outcomes. Act simply for the sake of action, deeply rooted in a compassionate love for all beings and non-beings.

At this moment, you are on a remarkable journey—honor and respect it. There is no eternal damnation as we traditionally conceive it. Your best strategy? Sit down, pull up a chair, and just breathe. Watch your breath as though observing the slowest clouds drift by. Ever watched a sloth? Embrace the fun challenge: be a sloth for a day. Slow down substantially. Feel every moment, immerse in it, absorb it, and let it stew. Notice the insights that surface when you reduce your pace and truly connect with your surroundings.

As we wrap up this journey, carry with you the light of those quiet, contemplative moments, the slow and steady pace of a sloth, and the luminous truths that emerge in darkness. Let these guide your path and inspire others long after our stories are shared. Here's to finding enlightenment not by racing to the finish line, but by savoring every step, every breath, every pause along the way.

You have all the time in the world. You are eternal. Honestly, whether you actively engage in this process or not, you will inevitably partake in it. Do what you can in this lifetime and then relax. If you're tired or depressed, just relax—there's nothing you must do but simply be. Don't push yourself too hard. You are perfect, exactly where you are meant to be.

Summary

Summary of Key Concepts

As we stand at the terminus of our exploration into the intricate web of Hermetic philosophy, it becomes evident that these ancient teachings remain as relevant today as they were millennia ago. Each principle, each insight, draws us closer to understanding the enigma of our existence and the vast universe we inhabit.

Throughout our journey, we've witnessed how the Hermetic doctrines provide a roadmap for personal and spiritual growth. From the boundless reaches of the Mental Universe to the rhythmic dance of Cause and Effect, we've navigated the dynamic interplay between our inner worlds and the vast cosmos.

Life, as we've come to understand, is not a mere series of random events. Instead, it's a symphony—a harmonious orchestra of energies, vibrations, and principles that guide our every thought, action, and emotion. The key to understanding this symphony lies not in seeking answers externally but in turning our gaze inward, to the vast universe within each of us. As we navigate through life's trials, elations, heartaches, and victories, it becomes clear that these are not mere individual encounters. Instead, they are vital steps in the grand ballet of the cosmos.

In essence, Hermetic philosophy doesn't just offer knowledge; it provides wisdom. Knowledge might inform our choices, but wisdom transforms our perspective, elevating our understanding of life's intricate web.

Let us conclude our enlightening journey by revisiting the pivotal landmarks that have shaped our understanding.

Techniques for Mental Transmutation

Throughout our exploration of Hermetic wisdom, practical techniques emerge as powerful tools to harness the mind's potential and bring about transformation. Delving into the realm of mental transmutation, certain methods stand out in their efficacy and simplicity:

1. **Visualization**: Imagining the desired state or outcome.

2. **Affirmation**: Repeating positive phrases to overwrite negative thought patterns.

3. **Mindfulness**: Being present to recognize and intercept undesirable thoughts.

4. **Breathwork**: Using controlled breathing to calm the mind and facilitate change.

Daily Practices for Ethical Living

In weaving the teachings of Hermeticism into the fabric of our daily lives, the focus often shifts from grand philosophies to tangible practices. These practices not only shape our actions but deeply enrich our ethical compass, guiding us towards harmonious living:

1. **Self-Reflection**: Taking time to introspect and understand one's intentions.

2. **Mindfulness**: Being aware of one's actions and their potential effects.

3. **Accountability**: Taking responsibility for one's actions, and making amends when necessary.

4. **Compassion**: Practicing empathy and understanding towards both oneself and others is essential because they are fundamentally interconnected. This realization will come in the state of the observer, when you will recognize that the observer and the observed are one.

Wisdom and the Seven Hermetic Principles

Rooted in the heart of Hermetic teachings, the Seven Hermetic Principles offer profound insights that, when internalized, translate to wisdom in action. Each principle serves as a lens, providing clarity and perspective in navigating the complexities of existence:

1. **Mentalism**: Wisdom involves the right use of the mind, understanding that "All is Mind."

2. **Correspondence**: It requires recognizing the interconnectedness of all things—"As above, so below."

3. **Vibration**: Wisdom includes the awareness of the vibrational nature of reality.

4. **Polarity**: It involves the understanding of opposites and the ability to reconcile them.

5. **Rhythm**: Wisdom calls for recognizing the cyclical nature of events and preparing for them.

6. **Cause and Effect**: Wise actions consider the repercussions and are made with foresight.

7. **Gender**: Wisdom understands the creative power inherent in the balance of masculine and feminine energies.

Across the realms of mental transmutation, ethical living, and the profound wisdom encapsulated in the Seven Hermetic Principles, we find a cohesive mosaic of guidance. These actionable techniques, daily practices, and timeless principles intertwine, creating a roadmap for the seeker. They beckon us toward higher consciousness, harmonious living, and deeper understanding, ensuring that our journey within the vast cosmos of Hermetic philosophy is not only enlightening but also deeply transformative.

Final Thoughts

As French philosopher Pierre Teilhard de Chardin astutely remarked,

> "We are not human beings having a spiritual experience; we are spiritual beings having a human experience."

This insightful reflection brings us full circle to the heart of Hermetic philosophy and the essence of the first section of this book.

In our exploration of the intricate fabric of Hermetic philosophy, we recognize that our journey is ceaseless. We've ventured deep into various Hermetic concepts: the core principles like Mentalism, Correspondence, Vibration, Polarity, Rhythm, Cause and Effect, and Gender, as well as the profound triad model of the human being encompassing body, soul, and spirit. Each of these is not an end, but a beacon, guiding us on a boundlessly vast and detailed spiritual quest.

Socrates once enlightened us with the words,

> "The only true wisdom is in knowing you know nothing."

Amid the vast expanse of the cosmos, our grasp is merely a speck. The genuine Hermetic disciple remains an eternal student, forever receptive to the profound enigmas of life.

Although the Hermetic journey is deeply intimate, it's not an isolated path. Pursue fellow seekers, mentors, or groups where experiences can be exchanged, and collective growth can transpire. Through the synergy of unified consciousness, our individual pursuits become boundlessly potent.

Central to Hermetic wisdom is the understanding of life's intrinsic interconnectivity. Navigate your spiritual trajectory with an expansive heart and mind. Embracing compassion and understanding not only serve as noble values but also as pivotal channels to the Divine.

True exploration of the self and the cosmos doesn't arise from stagnation within familiar terrains. It demands audacity, reminiscent of Anais Nin's reflection,

> "And the day came when the risk to remain tight in a bud was more painful than the risk it took to blossom."

Such bold leaps, be they through intensive study, pragmatic application, or service, are indispensable.

Aligning one's soul with the Divine is a ceaseless endeavor—a daily ritual of deliberate existence, perpetually aspiring for greater comprehension while infusing acquired knowledge into everyday practices.

In the eloquent words of Søren Kierkegaard,

> "To dare is to lose one's footing momentarily. Not to dare is to lose oneself."

Navigating the intricate pathways of spiritual enlightenment is by no means an easy endeavor. The terrain can be rugged, the valleys deep, and the peaks soaring. But within this challenging landscape, there are moments of reprieve, pockets of serenity, and spaces where you can pause, reflect, and rejuvenate. As you continue on, harnessing courage and determination, take solace in these frequent resting places. And as you strive towards higher understanding and deeper connection, remember the timeless wisdom from the Kybalion:

> "The ALL is Infinite Living Mind–the Illumined call it SPIRIT!"

As you conclude this section, and ideally embrace the tenets of Hermeticism, venture into the unknown. Dare to ponder, to journey, to embody authenticity, and to pursue Divine harmony. You encapsulate both the quest and its end, the apprentice and the sage. The forthcoming journey is uniquely yours, illuminated by the age-old insights of Hermeticism. May your voyage be abundant, your spirit dauntless, and your essence eternally resonate with the Divine.

As we tie the bow on this section, remember: being your own best friend isn't just a nice sentiment; it's the ultimate declaration of independence. Taking it further, being your own lover is the sequel where the plot thickens and the adventure deepens. And as for shaking hands with your inner universe—well, that's the secret handshake that grants you entry into the most exclusive club: genuine, unadulterated self-love and acceptance.

In this chaotic, beautiful mess of existence, may you find the courage to dance in the dark, to be the light when the sun hides, and to realize that every step, stumble, and pirouette is part of the most beautiful dance of all—the dance of being wonderfully, wildly, and whimsically you.

Now, let the music play, and let's dance until dawn under the starlit sky of our own making. Remember, one comes before two, so love and accept yourself first. This enables you to love and accept others. Also, remember that one and two are ultimately the same, and in the end, there is no two, just one and No One.

Section II

The Demiurge and the Hidden God

Introduction

What is This Section About?

Welcome to the second part of the book, designed to guide you through the fascinating concept of the Demiurge—a term that has intrigued thinkers, theologians, and scholars for centuries. At its core, the Demiurge is a primal creator figure, responsible for the formation of the physical universe. This part aims to unravel the complexity surrounding this mysterious figure, providing you with a clear and concise understanding of what the Demiurge is, how the concept has evolved, and its significance in various religious and philosophical systems.

As ancient Greek philosopher Socrates said,

"The unexamined life is not worth living."

The quote by Socrates captures the essence of why a section like this matters. Understanding concepts like the Demiurge enriches our worldview, offering us new perspectives on the nature of existence, creation, and perhaps even the meaning of life.

Who Should Read This Section?

This section is intended for anyone curious about metaphysical concepts, the origins of the universe, or the overlapping realms of philosophy and spirituality. You do not need any prior knowledge of these topics to understand the contents of this part. Whether you're a student, a spiritual seeker, or just someone interested in expanding your intellectual horizons, this section aims to offer something of value to you.

As Lewis Carroll famously penned in "Alice's Adventures in Wonderland,"

"Begin at the beginning," the King said gravely, "and go on till you come to the end: then stop."

Before we go further, let's explore what an **archetype** is and the importance of **symbolism** in the human psyche.

An archetype is like a universal pattern or model that exists in what's called the "collective unconscious"—a sort of shared mental and emotional warehouse where common human experiences and memories are stored. This collective unconscious is not something we are directly aware of; rather, it influences our thoughts and behaviors. Archetypes are templates that appear in stories, dreams, and myths across different cultures and times, representing familiar characters or scenarios that we all recognize instinctively, such as the Hero, the Wise Old Man, or the Nurturing Mother.

Symbolism, on the other hand, involves using symbols—objects, figures, or colors—to represent deeper ideas or qualities. For example, a dove often symbolizes peace, and a dark forest might represent the unknown or fear. Symbolism helps us connect with complex concepts on an emotional and intuitive level, enriching our understanding of ourselves and the world around us.

By using archetypes and symbols, writers tap into a shared human experience, creating stories that resonate deeply and evoke a powerful emotional response. These tools help weave narratives that feel both timeless and deeply personal, inviting readers to reflect on their own inner worlds and the mysteries beyond.

This introductory chapter serves to prepare you for the journey ahead. We'll start with the basics—defining what the term "Demiurge" means—and gradually delve deeper into its historical roots, its place in various philosophical discourses, and its significance in modern-day thought. We will also address controversies and debates surrounding the Demiurge, and by the end of this section, equip you with enough understanding to embark on your own exploration of this concept.

Now, let's begin this enlightening journey.

Defining Demiurge

Basic Definition

The word "Demiurge" comes from the Greek term "demiourgos," which translates to "worker" or "artisan." In its most basic sense, the Demiurge is understood as a creator deity or force responsible for crafting the material world. But, as you'll soon discover, the concept isn't as straightforward as it seems at first glance.

As stated in "The Apocryphon of John,"

> "The archon [Demiurge] said to his subjects, 'I am God, and there is no other God beside me.'"

This Gnostic quote sheds light on the complexity of the Demiurge's character. While seen as a creator, in Gnostic traditions the Demiurge also comes across as a being that claims divinity for itself, diverting souls from recognizing the higher, true divinity.

Origin of the Term

The term Demiurge has its roots in ancient Greek philosophy, notably in the works of Plato. However, it's essential to recognize that the concept predates Plato and has been a part of human cosmological theories across various cultures and epochs. Its name and nature may vary, but the core idea remains—there exists a being or force that has crafted the physical reality we inhabit.

As Galileo Galilei astutely observed,

> "Names and attributes must be accommodated to the essence of things, and not the essence to the names, since things come first and names afterwards."

Galileo's quote reminds us that while the term "Demiurge" is particular to specific philosophical and religious traditions, the underlying concept of a creator is nearly universal. This also suggests that our exploration should not be restricted merely to the nomenclature but should extend to the essence it aims to capture.

Multi-Faceted Interpretations

As we will see in the coming chapters, the Demiurge is not universally understood or described in the same way across different traditions. In some, it's a benevolent architect working to manifest a divine blueprint. In others, it's a somewhat flawed or even malevolent being who traps souls in the material world.

As Oscar Wilde succinctly put it,

"To define is to limit."

Wilde's words caution us as we delve deeper into defining the Demiurge. While it is crucial to offer clear definitions, we must remain aware that such definitions are often not all-encompassing. Our understanding will evolve as we journey through the various philosophical and spiritual landscapes that have engaged with this enigmatic concept.

In summary, the term "Demiurge" can be thought of as an artisan or creator responsible for the material universe. It originates from ancient philosophical discussions but has been adapted and reinterpreted across various religious and philosophical systems. Despite the various ways it is portrayed, the Demiurge remains a compelling concept for understanding the origins and organization of the world around us. As we proceed, we will explore these multiple facets in greater detail, always remembering that our definitions, while useful, may not fully encapsulate the complexity of what the Demiurge has represented through the ages.

Now that you have a basic understanding of what the Demiurge is, let's delve into its historical origins and how different philosophies and religions have conceptualized it.

Historical Overview

Ancient Greece

Ancient Greek philosophy is like the granddaddy of all Western thought. It laid the foundations for many ideas that we still talk about today, such as justice, beauty, and even the nature of existence. One of the big-name philosophers from ancient Greece is Plato, and he came up with a very intriguing concept—the Demiurge.

Plato was an ancient Greek philosopher who lived around 400 BC. He wrote a lot of dialogues, which are kind of like play scripts, where characters discuss big ideas. One of these dialogues is called "Timaeus," and it's here that he first talks about the Demiurge.

In "Timaeus," Plato describes the Demiurge as a "divine craftsman." Imagine a master artist or a skilled carpenter, but for the whole universe! According to Plato, this Demiurge took a look at the world when it was all chaotic and messy. He then used his "divine crafting skills" to organize this chaos into the world as we know it.

Plato suggests that the Demiurge uses a kind of heavenly blueprint to create the world. This blueprint is what Plato calls the "World of Forms." Basically, it's a realm of perfect, unchanging ideas or "forms" that the Demiurge uses as a guide for making the physical world.

Let's say you want to build the perfect chair. You'd have an idea of what that perfect chair should look like, right? In Plato's thinking, that "perfect chair idea" exists in the "World of Forms," and the Demiurge would use that ideal form as a model to create actual, physical chairs in our world.

As the ancient Greek philosopher Plato observed,

> "Reality is created by the mind, we can change our reality by changing our mind."

Although this quote isn't directly about the Demiurge, it helps us understand Plato's point. The Demiurge shapes the reality of the physical world based on ideal forms—much like how our minds can shape our own realities based on our ideas, beliefs, and perspectives.

Gnosticism

Gnosticism is a collection of religious ideas and systems that originated in the early Christian era. It's not a single organized religion, but rather a term that encompasses various beliefs that share some common themes. One such theme is a distinct view of the Demiurge, different from what Plato described.

In Gnostic texts, the Demiurge is often portrayed as an entity that is less than benevolent and sometimes downright malevolent. This is a big contrast to Plato's more positive, craftsman-like Demiurge. In Gnosticism, the Demiurge is often seen as a being who creates the physical world to trap human souls and keep them away from their true divine nature.

According to Gnostic belief, the Demiurge thinks it is the ultimate God and wants to keep human souls entrapped in the material world, ignorant of their true divine nature. It's like a cosmic con artist trying to divert us from realizing our true potential and spiritual heritage.

As recounted in The Apocryphon of John, the archon, or Demiurge, proclaimed,

> "I am God, and there is no other God beside me."

This quote illustrates the Demiurge's arrogance and misunderstanding of its place in the cosmic order. It believes itself to be the ultimate God, when in Gnostic belief, it is actually an inferior deity far removed from the true source of divinity.

As stated by Jesus Christ in the Gospel of Luke,

> "The kingdom of God is within you."

Though not a Gnostic text, this quote from the Gospel of Luke encapsulates a core Gnostic belief: the true divine source is within each of us, and it is not the Demiurge who creates the physical world. The material world, according to Gnosticism, is a distraction or even a trap that keeps us from recognizing and accessing our inner divinity.

By understanding both the Platonic and Gnostic views, you can see how the concept of the Demiurge has evolved and taken on different shades of meaning over time. While Plato saw it as a divine craftsman doing its best to create a good world, Gnostic texts often view it as a being that entraps and deceives. The Gnostic Demiurge serves as a warning—a cosmic red flag—signaling us to look inward for the divine rather than getting lost in the material world.

Neoplatonism

Neoplatonism is a philosophical system that emerged several centuries after Plato, building upon and extending his ideas. It was developed primarily by philosophers like Plotinus, who aimed to synthesize various strands of philosophy into a cohesive worldview.

Plotinus was an ancient philosopher who lived in the 3rd century AD. He's the main figure associated with Neoplatonism, and he brought some new ideas to the table regarding the Demiurge.

In Neoplatonic thought, the Demiurge is seen as an "emanation" from the "One." Think of the "One" as the ultimate source of everything, so pure and so perfect that it's beyond our comprehension. An emanation is like a natural outflow from this source—similar to how light emanates from the sun.

The Demiurge, in this view, is not an independent or separate being but rather a necessary aspect of the cosmic order. It serves as a link, connecting the ultimate unity of the One to the multiplicity and diversity of the material world.

In Neoplatonism, the universe is like a multi-layered cake. At the top, you have the "One," which is pure and perfect. As you go down the layers, things get more complex and less perfect. The Demiurge is essential because it acts as a mediator, translating the perfection of the "One" into the imperfect, material world we experience every day.

As the ancient philosopher Plotinus declared,

"All is One, One is All."

This quote encapsulates the essence of Neoplatonic thought. It tells us that everything is connected in a grand, unified whole. Even the Demiurge, which may be seen as a separate entity in other philosophies or religious traditions, is part of this unity in Neoplatonism. It's not an independent craftsman or a malevolent deceiver but a natural part of the cosmic process that connects the One to our material reality.

In summary, the concept of the Demiurge has a varied and complex history, changing dramatically depending on the philosophical or religious context. From the benevolent craftsman in Plato's vision to the misguided or malevolent creator in Gnostic texts, and finally as an integral part of the cosmic order in Neoplatonism, the Demiurge serves as a focal point for various ideas about the origins and structure of the universe. As we proceed, we will dive deeper into these varying interpretations and how they have shaped our understanding of reality.

Philosophical Context

Plato's Timaeus

In Plato's philosophy, the Demiurge is not a god to be worshipped in the way that traditional gods in polytheistic or monotheistic religions are. Instead, it's considered a "metaphysical principle," which means it's an essential part of the framework that explains how the universe or reality functions.

The term "eternal craftsman" is used to indicate that the Demiurge is an everlasting principle that is always active in shaping and maintaining the physical world. Unlike gods in mythologies who might rest after creating the world, this craftsman is eternally active, constantly working to maintain the balance and order of the cosmos.

In Plato's philosophy, there exists a realm of "Forms" or "Ideas," which are the perfect, unchanging archetypes of all things in the physical world. For instance, the Form of a circle is the concept of a perfect circle that exists only in the realm of Forms, and all circles in the physical world are approximations of this perfect circle. The Demiurge looks to these perfect Forms when creating or shaping the material world.

The quote from Plato,

> "Truth is the beginning of every good thing, both to gods and men; and he who would be blessed and happy should be from the first a partaker of truth,"

underscores the Demiurge's mission to replicate the ultimate truth found in the realm of Forms. This "ultimate truth" is the perfection or ideal state of being that the Forms represent. By attempting to replicate these Forms in the material world, the Demiurge is essentially trying to bring this ultimate truth into the realm of the physical.

It's worth noting that the Demiurge works within the "constraints of the physical world." This means that while the Demiurge aims to replicate the perfection of the Forms, it can't make the physical world entirely perfect. The material world is inherently flawed and limited, so it can never be a perfect replica of the realm of Forms.

By understanding these components, the passage argues that in Plato's philosophical system, the Demiurge is a principle of order and goodness. It serves to connect the perfect, unchanging world of Forms with the imperfect, constantly changing material world, continually striving to make the latter as close to the former as possible.

The Role of Demiurge in the Creation of the Universe

In philosophical discourse, the Demiurge often serves as a middle-ground entity between the realm of unchanging truths and the ever-fluctuating material world. It acts as a bridge or intermediary, crafting the universe with both design and purpose.

As Peter Drucker said,

"The best way to predict your future is to create it."

This sentiment serves as a powerful reminder that we are not merely passive participants in our own lives. Instead, we have the ability to actively shape our future through the decisions we make and the actions we take today.

Although Drucker's quote is aimed at personal development and not directly related to the Demiurge, the sentiment still holds value, it elegantly captures the role of the Demiurge in the philosophical context: as a being whose function is not just to predict or foresee, but to create, to bring forth the future (or in this case, the material world) based on a higher design or blueprint.

Is the Demiurge Good or Evil?

The morality of the Demiurge is a topic of much debate in philosophical circles. In Platonic and Neoplatonic thought, the Demiurge is inherently good or at least neutral, striving to mirror the perfection of the Forms. However, in Gnostic texts, the Demiurge often appears as ignorant or even malevolent, unaware of any higher reality beyond the physical world it has created.

As William Shakespeare insightfully noted in Hamlet,

"There is nothing either good or bad, but thinking makes it so."

Shakespeare's classic line can offer a fresh perspective on the moral ambiguity surrounding the Demiurge. The interpretation of the Demiurge's nature—whether it's good, evil, or something in between—often lies in the worldview of the interpreter rather than any intrinsic qualities of the Demiurge itself.

In this chapter, we've delved deep into the philosophical roots of the Demiurge, exploring its origins and roles from Plato's dialogues to Neoplatonist thought. We've seen how the Demiurge serves as a key principle that strives to bridge the ideal and the material worlds, working within the constraints of the latter to manifest the perfection of the former.

This philosophical framework not only sheds light on the complex nature of existence but also sets the stage for understanding how these abstract concepts are represented in symbolic forms. As we transition to the next chapter, we will examine the various symbols that have been associated with the Demiurge across different cultures and religious traditions. This will offer another layer of depth to our understanding, providing visual and symbolic dimensions to this complex entity.

Symbols of the Demiurge

The Language of Symbols

Symbols are more than mere decorations or simple illustrations; they are, as Swiss psychologist Carl Jung said,

> "the best possible expression of a thought that can never be completely elucidated."

This profound statement acknowledges that symbols serve as a language, one that can convey complex and often abstract ideas that may be too nuanced or vast for words alone. In the case of the Demiurge, this entity is not just an abstract concept confined to philosophical discourses and religious texts. Rather, it has been vividly portrayed through a myriad of symbols, each attempting to encapsulate its diverse nature and functions.

But why are symbols so important? Humans have an innate tendency to understand the world through the use of symbolism. Symbols help shape our understanding of the complex, often abstract, realities that words alone can't fully capture. From religious icons to national flags, symbols have the power to evoke deep emotions, tell intricate stories, and even shape societies. Jung went further to suggest that symbols are deeply ingrained in the human psyche and that they serve as conduits connecting our conscious minds to the unconscious.

Now, let's try to explain the conscious and unconscious mind in simple words, and explore how symbols affect both.

The conscious mind is like the part of your mind that's in charge when you're awake and aware. It handles your day-to-day thoughts, decisions, and actions. You can think of it as the captain of a ship, steering your thoughts and being aware of what's happening around you.

The unconscious mind, on the other hand, is like the vast ocean beneath the ship, hidden from view. It contains all the feelings, thoughts, and memories that are outside of your conscious awareness. It's powerful and vast, influencing you in ways you might not be directly aware of, like your instincts, habits, and reactions.

Symbols come into play as a bridge between these two parts of your mind. They can communicate complex ideas from the unconscious to the conscious mind. For instance, a snake might just seem like a snake in a dream, but it could symbolize danger, knowledge, or transformation, depending on the context. This is because symbols speak the language of the unconscious mind, tapping into deeper meanings and emotions.

By understanding and interpreting these symbols, we can gain insight into what our unconscious mind is trying to tell us, affecting how we think, feel, and behave in our conscious life. Symbols have the power to trigger reflections, reveal hidden feelings, and even motivate change by connecting the depths of our unconscious with our everyday conscious thoughts.

So, what are the symbols that represent the Demiurge, and what do they tell us about this complex and multifaceted entity? In this chapter, we will explore these visual and symbolic dimensions, diving deep into the portrayals that have emerged across different cultures and religious doctrines. By understanding these symbols, we can add another layer to our comprehension of the Demiurge and its impact on human thought and spirituality.

Classical Representations

In ancient art and literature, the Demiurge is often portrayed as a craftsman with tools in hand, busy with the act of creation. This reflects the Demiurge's role as described in Plato's "Timaeus," where the entity is tasked with shaping the material world.

As the Roman poet Horace eloquently put it,

"A picture is a poem without words."

The imagery of a craftsman serves as a "poem" that encapsulates the Demiurge's essence, presenting a vivid picture of its creative and formative power.

Gnostic Interpretations

In the realm of Gnostic thought, the Demiurge is often portrayed in a less than flattering light, a far cry from the benevolent craftsman of Platonic ideology. One of the most striking symbols associated with the Gnostic Demiurge is the lion-headed serpent, a complex figure replete with layers of meaning.

As Philip K. Dick aptly noted,

> "The symbols of the divine show up in our world initially at the trash stratum."

In Gnostic art and literature, the lion-headed serpent often appears with additional celestial symbols: the sun situated behind its head, and occasionally, the moon and stars surrounding it. Each component contributes to the narrative that Gnosticism paints about the Demiurge.

The lion-headed serpent is a fusion of two creatures generally considered opposites in nature: the lion, often associated with nobility and courage, and the serpent, commonly linked to wisdom but also deceit. This duality encapsulates the Gnostic view of the Demiurge as a complex figure that is both creator and obstructor, one that both enlightens and deceives.

The sun behind the serpent's head represents illumination and the power that the Demiurge wields over the material realm. Yet, in Gnostic thought, this light is often considered a false or lesser light, a pale imitation of the true divine illumination.

The moon and stars accompanying the figure further enhance its complexity. In many spiritual traditions, the moon symbolizes the subconscious, or hidden aspects, while stars often signify potential or individuality. In the context of the Gnostic Demiurge, these celestial bodies serve to highlight the scope and complexity of the created world, as well as the illusion or 'Maya' that the Demiurge perpetuates.

Taken together, these symbols offer a rich meaning, aiming to capture the multi-faceted and often paradoxical nature of the

Demiurge as understood in Gnostic traditions. Each symbol serves as a kind of spiritual shorthand, conveying complex ideas about the Demiurge's role as both a creator and a force that keeps souls entangled in the material realm.

Jungian Archetypes

In Carl Jung's psychological framework, an archetype is a universal symbol or motif that recurs across different cultures and throughout history. These archetypes are not learned but are instead a part of the collective unconscious, a term that Jung used to describe the part of the unconscious mind that is shared by a society, a people, or all humankind. Archetypes embody fundamental human experiences, serving as basic building blocks of the psyche and contributing to how individuals understand and navigate the world.

Let's explore a little what the collective unconscious and archetype are, and how they relate to each other.

The collective unconscious is a concept developed by psychologist Carl Jung, referring to a part of the unconscious mind that is shared among all humans. It's like a psychological foundation containing all the experiences and knowledge we inherit from our ancestors. This includes fears, dreams, and instincts that aren't learned but are innate.

Archetypes are the building blocks or main components of the collective unconscious. They are universal, archaic symbols and images that derive from the collective unconscious and are the psychic counterpart of instinct. For example, the Mother archetype represents nurturing and protection across cultures, even though the specifics of how these qualities are represented can vary.

In simple terms, archetypes are to the collective unconscious what organs are to the body; they are essential components that make up the whole system. They shape how we see the world, influence our behaviors, and affect the roles we take on in our societies. By tapping into these archetypes, we connect with the deeper aspects of the human experience, bridging individual and collective human experiences.

As Carl Jung articulated,

> "The archetype is a tendency to form such representations of a motif—representations that can vary a great deal in detail without losing their basic pattern."

The collective unconscious, according to Jung, is a layer of the unconscious mind that is inherited and shared among all humans. It is not shaped by personal experiences; rather, it contains universal experiences and ideas that are common to all human beings, regardless of their cultural background. The collective unconscious holds these universal symbols or archetypes, which surface in art, dreams, and religions.

As Carl Jung observed,

> "The collective unconscious consists of the sum of the instincts and their correlates, the archetypes. Just as everybody possesses instincts, so he also possesses a stock of archetypal images."

Jung saw the Demiurge as a manifestation of what he termed the "Self" archetype, representing the organizing principle and the fountainhead of all other archetypes. The Demiurge in Jung's perspective is both an inner and an outer principle. Internally, it stands for the dynamic force that brings cohesion and unity to the individual psyche. Externally, it symbolizes the pattern or structure that imposes order on the external world.

Jung's idea of the Demiurge is rooted in dualities: creation and destruction, consciousness and unconsciousness, and individuality and collectivity. He did not see the Demiurge as a solely benevolent or malevolent figure but as a complex, multi-faceted archetype with a wide array of potential meanings.

As Carl Jung articulated,

> "The self is not only the centre, but also the whole circumference which embraces both conscious and unconscious; it is the centre of this totality, just as the ego is the centre of consciousness."

In a simplified manner, Carl Jung saw the Demiurge as a sort of "universal symbol" that exists in the back of everyone's mind, a part of what he called the "collective unconscious." Imagine the collective unconscious as a vast library of symbols and ideas that every person is born with, even if they don't know it. These symbols are like templates for understanding the world around us, and they show up in our dreams, stories, and religions.

Jung thought the Demiurge was one such symbol, a stand-in for the idea of creation and organization. It's not necessarily good or bad; instead, it represents the creative and sometimes chaotic forces that are at work both in the world and within ourselves. So when you read about the Demiurge in ancient myths or modern stories, you're actually tapping into a symbol that has deep roots in the human mind—a symbol that can help you explore big questions about how the world is organized and what your place in it might be.

By understanding the Demiurge as an archetype within the collective unconscious, Jung elevates the concept beyond a mere historical or religious idea. Instead, it becomes a living symbol, deeply embedded in the psyche of every individual, reflecting universal tensions between order and chaos, between the finite and the infinite.

By exploring Jung's comprehensive insights, we can better appreciate the multidimensional nature of the Demiurge, recognizing its role not just in religious and philosophical traditions but also in the deepest corners of the human psyche.

In this chapter, we have traversed the landscape of symbols to explore the Demiurge's multi-faceted nature. From ancient portrayals to Jungian archetypes, each form and symbol adds a layer of complexity and nuance to our understanding of this enigmatic figure.

As we've seen, symbols serve as the language that bridges the gap between the conscious and the unconscious, the individual and the collective, the human and the divine. These symbolic portrayals set the stage for our next inquiry, where we will delve into the scriptural accounts and religious texts that further shape and define the concept of the Demiurge.

It is here that we'll see how age-old traditions have incorporated this figure into their cosmologies, offering yet another lens through which to examine its impact and relevance.

At the end of this chapter, I would like to focus your attention on a few points which might not directly connect with the root subject of this book but are very important to put into your conscious thought. Just stop for a moment and think about how capitalism, big companies, and politicians use these symbols and archetypes to turn the tide in their favor. I am not saying what is good or bad—that is all beyond duality, at least for me anyway. But I would like my readers to think about this and, instead of being used by these forces, try to take actions consciously rather than being swayed by someone else's will. Always remember, action based on love and compassion is the highest form of act. Now, let's go to the next chapter.

Demiurge in Religious Texts

Demiurge in Gnostic Texts

In Gnostic traditions, the Demiurge often takes on a less flattering role compared to its Platonic counterpart. Here, the Demiurge is not the ultimate God but rather a lesser deity responsible for creating the physical, material world. The Gnostic Demiurge is generally seen as ignorant or even malevolent, blinding souls to their true, divine nature.

As stated in The Gospel of Thomas,

> "Know what is in front of your face, and what is hidden from you will be disclosed to you."

This quote from the Gnostic Gospel of Thomas encapsulates the Gnostic approach to the Demiurge. According to Gnostic texts, understanding the nature of the Demiurge leads to greater spiritual insights and frees one from the illusions of the material world.

Contrasting Yahweh and the Gnostic Demiurge

In exploring the character of the Demiurge, it's vital to understand its contrasting portrayals in different religious traditions. One of the most interesting comparisons is with Yahweh, the God of the Old Testament. Carl Jung, a renowned psychologist, had some thought-provoking insights on this subject.

Jung observed that Yahweh seemed to define himself through his creations, almost as if he needed them to confirm his own existence. He wasn't fully aware of himself in the way a human being with self-reflective capabilities might be. In simpler terms, imagine a painter so engrossed in his paintings that he forgets he is more than just the act of painting. This lack of self-awareness makes Yahweh act in ways that appear contradictory or confusing to humans.

According to Jung, this doesn't mean that Yahweh is bad or imperfect, like the Gnostic view of the Demiurge as a malevolent creator. Yahweh is, instead, a complex being who embodies all qualities, both good and bad. He is the totality of everything, which means he can be both completely just and its total opposite.

The idea is that Yahweh, unlike the Gnostic Demiurge, isn't limited to just one aspect of morality or creation. He's a more complex figure, embodying multiple traits and characteristics that may sometimes appear contradictory to us.

While we should bear in mind that these are interpretations shaped by human thought, they offer us unique windows into understanding the complex and multifaceted nature of divine entities like the Demiurge and Yahweh.

In summary, the complex nature of divine entities like Yahweh and the Demiurge demands a nuanced approach to understanding them. While the Gnostic Demiurge is often portrayed as a limited, even malevolent being, Yahweh presents a different picture—a being of multifaceted qualities, both just and unjust, aware and unaware.

Carl Jung's insights remind us that these deities can be seen as reflections of our own inner complexities and potentialities, not just as external figures. They embody contradictions that challenge our conventional understanding of morality, self-awareness, and divinity. Thus, the Demiurge and Yahweh serve as intriguing mirrors for exploring the intricate threads of both the divine and human psyche.

Similarities and Differences in Eastern Religions

Though the term "Demiurge" originates from Western traditions, one can identify analogous ideas within Eastern religious philosophies, particularly in Hinduism. In Hindu cosmology, Brahma is the god responsible for the act of creation. However, Brahma is not the ultimate reality; that designation belongs to Brahman, the unchanging, infinite, immanent, and transcendent reality amidst and beyond the world.

To better understand, consider Brahma as a craftsman and Brahman as the ultimate essence or the metaphysical clay from which the craftsman molds the world. While Brahma spins the web of the visible world, he is still an aspect of the overarching Brahman, the ultimate reality. In this way, Brahma serves a function similar to the Demiurge, as he too brings the physical world into existence but is not regarded as the supreme power.

The Bhagavad Gita, a 700-verse Hindu scripture, offers an insightful perspective on creation that aligns closely with this conversation. As the Bhagavad Gita proclaims,

"Creation is only the projection into form of that which already exists."

This quote speaks volumes about Eastern attitudes towards the concept of creation. Like the Demiurge, Brahma doesn't create the world from nothing; he shapes it from an already-existing higher reality, which is Brahman. This aligns well with the Platonic or Neoplatonic notion of the Demiurge fashioning the world as a reflection of pre-existing ideal Forms or as an emanation from the "One."

The concept of a creating entity similar to the Demiurge can vary significantly based on the religious or philosophical tradition one examines. In the Gnostic tradition, the Demiurge is often seen as a malevolent or ignorant entity that separates human souls from their divine source. In contrast, Hindu philosophy presents a more benign creator in Brahma, who nevertheless is not the ultimate source of divine truth.

In summary, while the term "Demiurge" may not appear explicitly in Eastern religions, the idea it encapsulates finds resonance in philosophies like Hinduism. Across varying religious landscapes, this enigmatic entity serves as a compelling model for exploring how different cultures and spiritualities navigate the profound questions of creation, divinity, and ultimate reality.

I would also like to clarify that I am not promoting any religion as superior to another; each person's spiritual journey is deeply personal. It is important to note that even within Hinduism, many adherents may not engage with the religion's teachings as originally intended, getting caught up in the symbolism which was meant to aid in understanding transcendence—the ultimate reality—not for mere worship but to grasp the indescribable absolute reality. I am not here to judge anyone, as each person's path is unique. Sooner or later, we all will find our place where consciousness leads us in this grand orchestration, the play of existence.

As we conclude this chapter, it becomes evident that the concept of the Demiurge, while rooted in Platonic philosophy, has found a multitude of expressions across different religious and philosophical systems. From the Gnostic portrayal of a malevolent jailer to the multifaceted, morally complex characterization in the Judeo-Christian tradition, and even to its analogous counterparts in Eastern philosophies like Hinduism, the Demiurge serves as a universal symbol for the tension between the ideal and the material, the ultimate and the immediate.

This exploration reveals the inherent human curiosity about the origins of existence, the nature of the divine, and our own role within the cosmic landscape. The Demiurge, in its various incarnations, invites us to question, ponder, and possibly reconfigure our understanding of these primal concerns. Each tradition we've examined adds a unique lens, widening our collective perspective on a concept that defies simple categorization. Whether viewed as a creator, a guardian, a trickster, or a psychological archetype, the Demiurge remains an endlessly intriguing figure that challenges us to think more deeply about the world we inhabit and the unseen realms that may lie beyond it.

By surveying the many religious texts that discuss or allude to the Demiurge, we've taken a comprehensive look at this elusive concept. Yet the journey is far from over, as each new generation revisits these ancient ideas, adding their own interpretations and insights. This ever-evolving dialogue ensures that the Demiurge will continue to be a subject of intrigue and debate, captivating the minds of seekers for generations to come.

As we reflect on the diverse interpretations of the Demiurge across various traditions, exploring its manifestations from malevolent creator to misunderstood deity, let us also consider a deeper, more universal contemplation of the Divine that transcends even these ancient texts and teachings, inviting us to ponder the infinite and ineffable nature of God.

The concept of God, in its myriad interpretations, has long been a cornerstone of human contemplation and spirituality. From the tangible, emotive descriptions of a Personal God to the abstract, boundless depictions of an Impersonal God—and even beyond these categorizations—the Divine remains an enigma, deeply personal and yet universally sought.

The famous theologian Paul Tillich once said,

> "God does not exist. He is being itself beyond essence and existence."

This quote encapsulates the ineffable nature of the Divine, suggesting that our attempts to define or understand God through conventional means or language might always fall short. Similarly, the ancient Hindu scriptures expound on the idea of 'neti-neti' (not this, not that), reminding seekers that any conceptualization of the Divine is but a mere approximation.

However, it is in this very exploration—a dance between knowing and unknowing—that many find profound spiritual growth. As Rumi, the celebrated Sufi poet, beautifully expressed,

> "Silence is the language of God; all else is poor translation."

Our narratives, whether of a Personal or Impersonal God, are attempts to translate this cosmic silence into something comprehensible, something relatable. But perhaps the true essence of God, as many mystics and philosophers suggest, lies in the journey itself, in the continuous quest for understanding, in the moments of doubt, in the epiphanies, and in the silent meditations.

It's a journey that celebrates not just the destination, but the path, the questions, the challenges, and the insights.

As Saint Augustine wisely observed,

"If you comprehend it, it is not God."

Thus, while we navigate the vast expanse of spiritual thought, it is vital to remain open, humble, and curious, recognizing that the Divine, in its infinite wisdom, might always remain a beautiful mystery, forever inviting, forever elusive.

It's only one, there's only one, it's all one. You can delve into physics, down to the quantum of energy, and reach a point where it's all one stuff—there's only one of it. One goes into many, and many of us busy thinking we are separate. After awakening, many start appreciating they are part of one, and they all come back into the one. And then, the interesting point is that the one includes the many.

You are without form, without limit, you are beyond space, beyond time, you are in everything, everything is in you, everywhere you are. That part of you I am, and that part of me you are, is the same; there's only one. Have compassion and love for yourself and others, as there's only one, and we are all going through this. Take life, death, pain, suffering as it is, and see it all as unfolding the laws, the law of forms, but who you are has no form, no limit.

All forms are within law; who you are is free, but who you think you are is within the law, your container is the lawful container, including your thinking mind. Everything you think is lawful, but everything that you are is beyond law. Take life as it is and love it as it is.

The Great Reveal

The Mirror of God

Carl Jung posited that,

> "Man is the mirror which God holds up to himself, or the sense organ with which he apprehends his being."

This profound statement opens up a realm of inquiry into how humans interact with the divine, both as reflections and as sensory instruments.

If we consider ourselves the "mirror" in which God sees His reflection, it implies that our existence serves as a means for the Divine to understand itself. In this regard, we become co-creators of the universe and are endowed with a purpose that far transcends mere existence; we become instrumental in the ongoing narrative of cosmic self-awareness.

Similarly, being the "sense organ" of the Divine suggests that human consciousness, with its complexities and potentials, serves a higher purpose. We're not passive spectators but active participants in a grand cosmic drama, our lives contributing to the divine understanding of existence and morality.

This makes the human experience not merely a byproduct of the Demiurge's creation but a critical component. "So-called progress," as Jung describes it, "leads simultaneously to a spiritual inflation and to an unconsciousness of God." Our technological and intellectual advancements might inflate our sense of importance, but they also distance us from the humility of recognizing our role as mere "sensors" in the divine scheme.

In Jung's view, human beings are not just passive creations of the Demiurge; we play an essential role in the divine plan. When we make progress—especially in technology and knowledge—we sometimes start to feel overly important. This 'spiritual inflation' can make us forget that we are, essentially, the 'sense organs' through which the divine understands itself. In other words, our advancements may make us proud, but they can also make us forget our true role in the grand scheme of things.

Inflating the Human Spirit

Carl Jung warned of the duality inherent in human progress, stating that it

> "leads simultaneously to a spiritual inflation and to an unconsciousness of God (genetivus accusativus!)."

On one hand, the marvels of technology, science, and human achievement have endowed us with an ever-expanding range of abilities that would have seemed miraculous just a few generations ago. Whether it's exploring outer space, modifying our genetic code, or creating complex virtual realities, our capacity to manipulate our environment and ourselves has grown exponentially.

However, this "progress" also carries with it a perilous form of spiritual "inflation." As we become more proficient masters of the material world, it's easy to forget the divine spark that, according to various philosophical and spiritual traditions, ignited the flame of human intelligence and creativity in the first place. In this sense, we become victims of our own success, allowing our technological and intellectual achievements to cloud our understanding of our relationship with the divine.

Jung's use of the term "genetivus accusativus" implies a grammatical relationship that is both possessive and accusative. This suggests that as we progress, we not only "possess" our achievements but are also "accused" by them, in the sense that they make us forget our foundational relationship with the Divine, and thus render us "unconscious of God."

In our quest for progress, we may confuse the tools and processes that we've created with the underlying realities they were designed to manipulate or understand. And herein lies the danger: when we mistake the map for the territory, we run the risk of thinking we are the creators rather than the created, further obscuring our understanding of the Demiurge and our role within the grand scheme of existence.

The Demiurge Within

In a letter, Carl Jung explored the intricate relationship between humanity and the divine, writing:

> "Man confuses himself with God, is identical with the demiurge and begins to usurp cosmic powers of destruction, i.e., to arrange a second Deluge."

In the ancient world, the concept of the Demiurge represented an intermediary between the human and the divine. As a lesser deity responsible for shaping the material world, the Demiurge was viewed as something separate from humankind. However, in our modern era, advancements in technology and philosophy have blurred this distinction.

We live in an age where the boundaries of human capability are continuously expanding. Whether it's mastering genetics, manipulating the weather, or inventing new forms of artificial intelligence, we're increasingly taking on roles once ascribed to gods or the divine. But what happens when we start to believe that we are not just mimicking the creative or destructive powers traditionally assigned to deities, but that we are those deities?

Jung suggests a dark potential for self-deception here. By claiming god-like powers—whether through technological advancements or ideological constructs—we risk identifying so fully with the Demiurge that we lose sight of our limitations. When this happens, we begin to "usurp cosmic powers of destruction," convinced that we're qualified to make sweeping changes to the natural order. Jung evokes the image of a "second Deluge," a catastrophic flood like the one described in ancient scriptures, to underline the dangers of this arrogance.

The consequences of confusing ourselves with God or the Demiurge are not merely philosophical musings; they could have tangible, disastrous implications. It's not just that we risk losing our ethical or spiritual bearings; we risk unleashing forces that we neither fully understand nor control, all while laboring under the illusion that we do.

To better understand these dynamics, it's crucial to explore the interplay between our expanding capabilities and our philosophical or spiritual understanding of what those capabilities mean. As we continue to push the boundaries of what is possible, we must also push the boundaries of our understanding, striving always to maintain a balanced view of our place in the grand cosmic scheme.

Cosmic Powers

Jung, in his letters, warned of the dangers when

> "Man... begins to usurp cosmic powers of destruction, i.e., to arrange a second Deluge."

This ominous caution is more than a metaphor; it's a direct confrontation with the perilous capabilities that we've accrued in the modern age.

Advancements in fields like nuclear physics, biotechnology, and artificial intelligence have vested humanity with capabilities that were once the exclusive domain of mythological gods or natural forces. We have the technological means to significantly alter or even destroy life on a planetary scale, mimicking the mythical "second Deluge" that Jung refers to.

While these advancements signify monumental achievements in human intelligence and creativity, they also embody an immense potential for destruction. The mastery over cosmic forces carries not just the promise of improving life but also the threat of annihilating it. Our newfound powers have outpaced our ethical and philosophical frameworks, leaving us susceptible to recklessness or misuse of these technologies.

The 'Demiurge within' isn't just a philosophical or metaphorical idea; it is a very real potential that could either elevate us to unprecedented heights or precipitate our downfall. Jung's warning thus serves as a sobering reminder that with great power comes not just great responsibility, but also great peril.

As we advance further into an era of unparalleled technological capability, it is incumbent upon us to exercise an equally advanced ethical discretion. In essence, it's not enough to possess the powers of a god; we must also cultivate the wisdom to wield them judiciously. Therefore, navigating this potential for destruction requires a deep understanding of both our capabilities and our limitations, in the pursuit of a more balanced, sustainable interaction with the world.

A Double-Edged Sword

Carl Jung emphasized the incredible existential risk that accompanies the concept of God becoming man. This transformation isn't just theological; it directly affects human psychology and society. Jung noted that the danger of "God becoming man" also threatens humanity with the notion of "becoming God," which can usher in a sense of cosmic hubris.

When humans blur the lines between the divine and the mortal, as evidenced by our advancements in technology, morality, and understanding of the universe, we encounter a paradox. On one hand, the closer we get to "becoming God," the greater our potential for creative, positive transformation. On the other hand, this same potential enables us to wield "cosmic powers of destruction," leading us to a path that could end in devastation.

Jung viewed this as a psychological and spiritual tightrope. The concept of becoming god-like is tantalizing but perilous. When imbued with a divine-like ability to create and destroy, humans have to manage the tension between these opposing forces carefully. The mistake lies in believing that we have tamed the chaos that comes with such power, thinking we've become masters of the universe rather than co-creators or stewards.

What further complicates the matter is our limited understanding of the "mysteria Dei," or the mysteries of God. If we were to truly comprehend the profound nature of divine powers, would we still be as eager—or as reckless—in wielding them? Or would a deeper understanding of these cosmic responsibilities humble us into more cautious action?

In summary, the danger of God becoming man is indeed a double-edged sword: it both empowers and endangers us. It is a cautionary tale of what could happen when we overestimate our abilities and underestimate the complexities of divine or cosmic responsibilities. We are at a crossroads where our next steps must be taken with an acute awareness of this profound, dualistic potential.

The Theological Balancing Act

Carl Jung's observation on the Catholic and Protestant approaches to faith adds another layer to our understanding of humanity's relationship with the divine. The Catholic Church, according to Jung, manages to balance belief and action through faith and ritual. This equilibrium serves as a safeguard against the dangers of "spiritual inflation," where humans might mistakenly equate themselves with God.

In Protestantism, the emphasis is mainly on "sola fide," or faith alone. This focus, while spiritually enriching, might leave individuals more susceptible to the psychological pitfalls of identifying too closely with the divine. Jung's contention here is that the act of faith itself can be both empowering and precarious.

Carl Jung delved into the nuanced interplay between faith and ritual in one of his letters, stating:

> "Sometimes semel credidisse is sufficient for him since he has the ritual graces,"

highlighting how a one-time act of faith may be enough when it's tempered by ritualistic practices.

The concept of ritual graces brings us to an interesting point: rituals act as both a manifestation and a grounding of faith. They help contain and channel the spiritual energies and enthusiasms evoked by faith. In doing so, rituals can serve as a psychological and spiritual "safety net," providing a structured way for individuals to interact with the divine without losing their grounding in the earthly realm.

Therefore, in the intricate dance between human and divine, faith and ritual serve as counterbalances. Faith propels us towards the divine, filling us with spiritual vigor and existential purpose. Rituals, on the other hand, tether us to earthly realities and responsibilities, reminding us that while we may strive for god-like wisdom and abilities, we are not gods ourselves. Thus, a balanced theological approach could act as a safety measure against the risks identified in the previous sections: that of humanity confusing itself with the divine and consequently wielding potentially destructive cosmic powers.

Given these insights, it becomes evident that a balanced theological approach is not just a theoretical ideal but a practical necessity. By harmonizing faith and ritual, one can not only deepen their spiritual experience but also protect themselves from the hubris of over-identifying with the divine. This equilibrium, then, serves as a mechanism that allows humans to explore the depth of their spirituality while remaining grounded in their human limitations. In a world where spiritual quests often lead to extreme ideologies and practices, the wisdom of balancing faith with ritual offers a tempered path that respects both the celestial and the terrestrial aspects of our existence.

Contemplating the Mysteria Dei

Jung urges us to "learn to understand the mysteria Dei better," emphasizing the importance of deepening our comprehension of divine mysteries. The term "mysteria Dei" refers to the incomprehensible aspects of God or the divine. By advocating for a better understanding of these mysteries, Jung is essentially calling for a more profound awareness of the complexities involved in the human-divine relationship.

Why is understanding these mysteries so crucial? The danger lies in our tendency to simplify what is inherently complex, and in doing so, create skewed representations of both man and God— possibly identifying one as the other. Such simplifications can lead us toward the dangerous path of over-identification with the divine, potentially resulting in destructive behavior.

If we don't comprehend the inherent complexities of the divine, we run the risk of making assumptions that oversimplify and limit our understanding of our place in the cosmos. This misunderstanding can, in turn, lead to the "unconsciousness of God," a state in which we, filled with our own sense of inflated importance, forget the divine aspects and complexities that are beyond human grasp.

Understanding the "mysteria Dei" calls for humility. It's a call to accept the limitations of human knowledge and capability while striving for a more profound understanding. This involves a careful balance between embracing our potential to reflect divine attributes, and maintaining a humble acceptance of our inherent limitations. In contemplating the mysteries of the divine, we create a protective barrier against the intoxicating and dangerous idea of ourselves as demiurges, thereby ensuring a healthier relationship with the realm of the divine.

Navigating the Thin Line Between Human and Divine

Navigating the delicate balance between our human limitations and divine potentialities is no simple task. As we've explored throughout this chapter, there's a seductive allure to elevating ourselves to the status of the Demiurge, particularly in an age of rapid technological and intellectual advancements. We stand on the precipice, armed with unprecedented powers of creation and destruction, all the while grappling with our limited understanding of divine complexities—the "mysteria Dei."

Jung warns us of the dangers of confusing man with God and of the intoxicating effects of "spiritual inflation." The task then is one of equilibrium—acknowledging our divine-like capabilities while remaining aware of our limitations. This requires a nuanced understanding of faith and ritual, as well as a cautious approach to interpreting religious and philosophical ideas about the Demiurge and divine creation.

The stakes are high. The implications of mistaking ourselves for the divine could unleash chaotic forces we neither comprehend nor control. Therefore, a careful, conscious understanding of our own capabilities and limitations is not just advisable, but essential.

In essence, we must strive for a respectful relationship with the divine, a relationship rooted in both awe and understanding. This is the safest way to navigate the perilous journey on the tightrope stretched between the human and the divine, ensuring that we neither fall into the abyss of destructive god-like pretensions nor lose sight of our remarkable human potential.

Navigating the Human-Divine Continuum

As we come to the close of this exploration into the complex and nuanced concept of the Demiurge—and particularly our consideration of humans as potential demiurges themselves—it's essential to ground our insights in everyday actions. While philosophical and theological inquiries provide us with a framework for understanding, they must ultimately translate into practical steps if they are to make a difference in the real world. In this section, we outline actionable solutions that allow us to better navigate the delicate balance between our human limitations and our demiurgic potential. By incorporating these strategies into our lives, we can engage more mindfully with our own abilities to create and destroy, thus honoring the divine complexity within us.

1. Self-Awareness and Reflection:

One of the central themes of this chapter is the demiurgic potential within humanity—that is, our capacity to be creators and destroyers. Self-awareness is critical in tempering this potential. Practice mindfulness and self-reflection to become more conscious of your actions and their broader implications.

2. Ethical Mindfulness:

Given the demiurgic potential in all of us, ethical mindfulness is crucial. Before making significant decisions, consider their moral and ethical dimensions. Ask yourself: "Am I acting out of a sense of egoic inflation, or am I genuinely contributing to the greater good?"

3. Balanced Faith:

As discussed in the sub-section on "Faith and Ritual: The Theological Balancing Act," striking a balance between belief and action is crucial. Whether you follow a religious path or a secular one, find a structured way to check your spiritual or ethical growth. This can be through rituals, moral codes, or ethical philosophies that serve as a counterbalance to unbridled ego.

4. Community Engagement:

Isolation can lead to an inflated sense of self, feeding the demiurge within. Engaging with a community allows you to gain perspectives other than your own, providing a kind of 'reality check' which can be both grounding and humbling.

5. Environmental Responsibility:

Given our 'cosmic powers of destruction,' it's essential to be responsible stewards of the Earth. Adopt sustainable practices in your daily life and advocate for policies that protect our planet. Our ability to create or destroy isn't just metaphysical; it has very tangible consequences for the Earth.

6. Education:

Invest in education that focuses not just on knowledge but also on emotional intelligence and ethical reasoning. An education system that addresses these aspects can better equip future generations to handle the power that comes with human progress responsibly.

7. Promote Dialogue:

The sub-section on "Contemplating the Mysteria Dei" emphasized the need for understanding. Foster dialogue between different religious, spiritual, and secular groups. It's only through understanding each other's perspectives that we can arrive at a balanced view of our place in the cosmos.

Being aware of our demiurgic potential is the first step in using it wisely. By applying these practical solutions, we can strive to walk the delicate line between human and divine, fulfilling our creative potential while remaining grounded in ethical and communal responsibility.

By being cautious stewards of our immense potential, we not only respect the divine aspects within us but also ensure that they are channeled constructively for the benefit of all.

In conclusion, I would like to emphasize the importance of releasing the need to have all the answers. We don't—and can't—know everything. The most profound approach we can take is to allow the life force to flow through us, letting the universe carry out its work while actively participating as co-creators. Much like the Demiurge, who shapes form from formlessness, we too sculpt our reality through our thoughts, bringing ideas from the realm of the intangible into the material world. This dynamic process invites us to not just be passive observers but engaged creators, molding our existence with conscious intention.

Ultimately, we will find ourselves exactly where we started, precisely where we are meant to be. So relax, breathe deeply, and take comfort in knowing that you are safe within the vast expanse of the cosmos, actively contributing to its unfolding.

The Human Journey

As we conclude our exploration of the Demiurge, it is imperative to bring our attention back to the very beings entangled in this cosmic narrative—us, human beings. Carl Jung, whose insights have informed much of this section, left us with profound thoughts that resonate deeply when contemplating our role in this intricate web of creation and perception.

Carl Jung, made an insightful observation about the varying responsibilities of self-focus at different stages of life. He stated:

> "For a young person, it is almost a sin, or at least a danger, to be too preoccupied with himself; but for the ageing person, it is a duty and a necessity to devote serious attention to himself."

The journey with the Demiurge invites us to reflect on the inner and outer worlds we inhabit. It beckons us to give 'serious attention' to our place within the grand scheme, especially as we age and grow in wisdom.

As we move forward in our lives, the questions surrounding the Demiurge are not just intellectual curiosities but have real implications for our spiritual well-being. In discussing the psychological and spiritual needs of individuals, particularly those in the latter stages of life, Carl Jung made an eye-opening statement. He observed,

> "I have treated many hundreds of patients. Among those in the second half of life – that is to say, over 35 – there has not been one whose problem in the last resort was not that of finding a religious outlook on life."

The notion of the Demiurge can offer a lens through which to explore this 'religious outlook,' understanding our complexities and contradictions as reflective of something much greater than ourselves.

Finally, Jung gives us reason to appreciate the full arc of human life. As a final thought, Carl Jung offers a compelling perspective on the value and significance of aging, emphasizing that the latter years of human life are not to be seen as mere continuations of youth but should be appreciated for their own unique meaning. As Jung said,

"A human being would certainly not grow to be seventy or eighty years old if this longevity had no meaning for the species. The afternoon of human life must also have a significance of its own and cannot be merely a pitiful appendage to life's morning."

The idea of the Demiurge and the dialogues it provokes serve not just as philosophical musings, but as guiding lights that can illuminate the 'afternoon of human life,' allowing us to see it as an invaluable part of a greater cosmic drama.

By engaging with the concept of the Demiurge, we embark on a journey that enriches our understanding not only of the world around us but also the inner landscape of our souls. It is a journey that can add depth and dimension to every stage of human life, from the exuberance of youth to the reflective quietude of age.

As we draw this section to a close, I leave you with a poignant quote from the Bhagavad Gita:

"Free from all thoughts of 'I' and 'mine', man finds absolute peace."

This timeless wisdom invites us to transcend our egos, to release the attachments that bind us, and to embrace a state of peace that is both profound and liberating.

In this journey, let love and compassion be your guiding stars. These virtues not only enrich our own lives but also illuminate the paths of others around us. As we navigate the complexities of existence, let us remember that at the core of all spiritual seeking is the pursuit of a deeper, more connected experience of love and compassion—toward ourselves, toward others, and toward the universe itself.

May you carry the insights and inspirations from these pages into your daily life, and may you find joy in the continual unfolding of your own spiritual path. Thank you for sharing this journey with me. Be at peace, and remember, you are always held safely within the boundless love of the cosmos.

Section III

Alchemical Training

Introduction

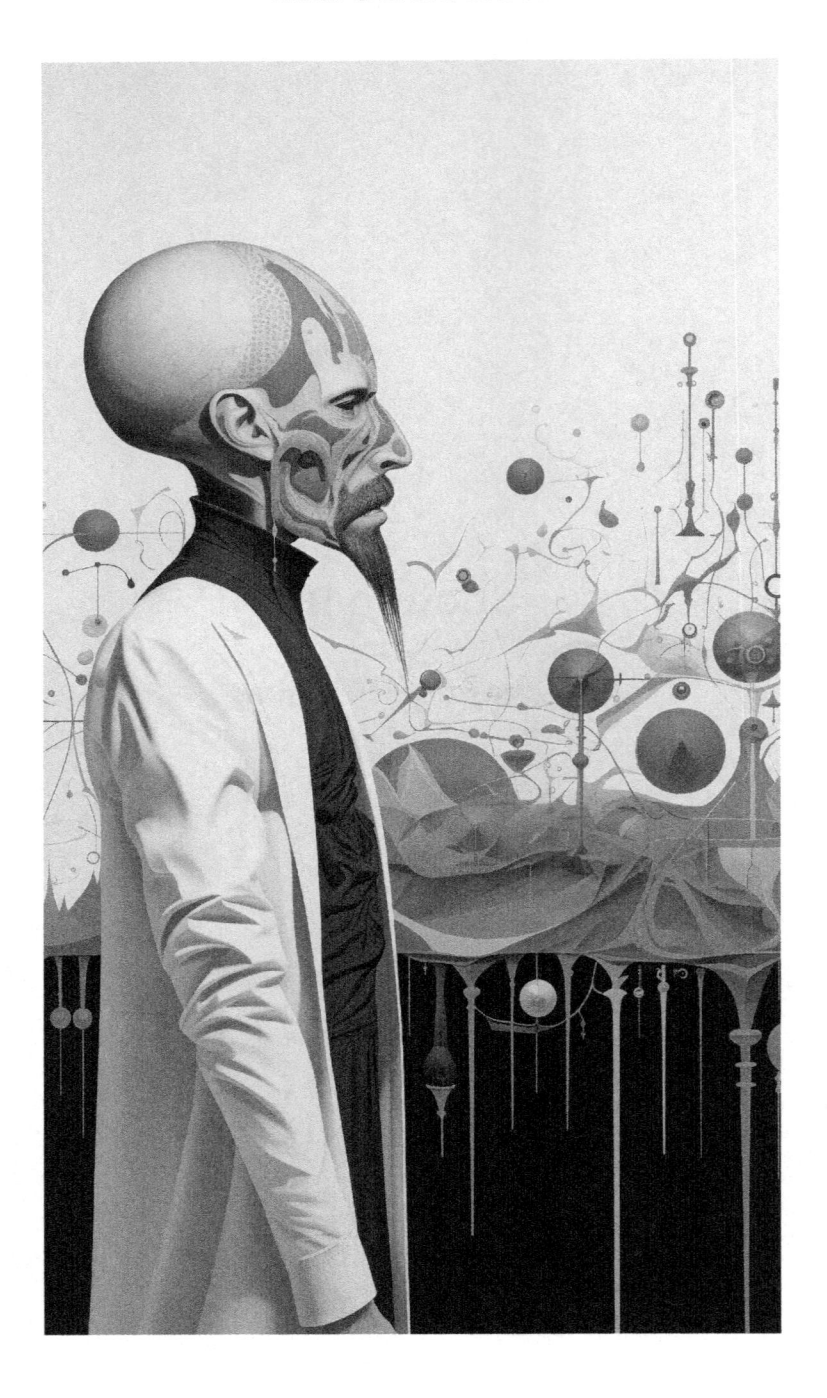

The Human Mind

The human mind, a marvel of nature, has captivated thinkers, scientists, and philosophers for centuries. It is this intricate nexus of thoughts, emotions, and memories that defines who we are, how we perceive the world, and how we react to it. Yet, while we often think we are at the mercy of our thoughts and feelings, ancient teachings have illuminated the possibility of harnessing and transforming the very fabric of our consciousness. This journey, dear reader, is nothing short of the great alchemical work, an inner transmutation, where base thoughts are turned into golden beliefs that empower and elevate.

To embark on this voyage, we must first understand the landscape of our mind. Traditionally, the mind is understood to operate on two primary levels: the Conscious and the Subconscious. The Conscious mind is our day-to-day awareness, the thoughts we actively think, the decisions we make, and the sensations we perceive. It's the tip of the iceberg, visible and tangible.

Beneath this surface lies the vast expanse of the Subconscious mind, a reservoir of beliefs, memories, and feelings. The ancient Hermeticists saw this as the realm of potential, where the seeds of our destiny lie dormant, waiting for the alchemist's touch to awaken and transform.

"As within, so without. As above, so below",

teaches the Hermetic axiom, indicating that our external reality is but a reflection of our inner beliefs and perceptions.

If we are to change our external circumstances, we must first embark on the great work of reshaping our inner world. And herein lies the magic of affirmations. Affirmations are not mere words; they are potent spells, declarations to the universe, and, most importantly, to our Subconscious mind. Repeated with conviction and emotion, they have the power to rewrite our internal narratives, replacing limiting beliefs with empowering truths.

The ancient Greek philosopher, Socrates, profoundly stated,

> "To know thyself is the beginning of wisdom."

The final section of this book invites you on a transformative journey. As you traverse its chapters, you'll encounter powerful affirmations designed to align your Subconscious with your highest aspirations. But remember, alchemy is not a passive process. Just as the alchemist must tend to his crucible, you must actively engage with these affirmations, allowing them to seep into your Subconscious, replacing the old with the new.

We stand at the precipice of a new era, one where the ancient teachings of Hermeticism and the promise of alchemy can guide us in reshaping our reality from the inside out. This is your call to the great work, a work that begins within and has the power to reshape not just your reality but the world.

The enlightened sage, Buddha, once proclaimed,

> "The mind is everything. What you think, you become."

In the mystical fabric of Hermetic teachings, there exists a foundational principle that declares,

> "The ALL is Mind; The Universe is Mental."

This profound axiom asserts that everything, from the vastness of the cosmos to the intricacies of our thoughts, emanates from a singular, universal mind. It's this shared mental fabric that binds us, makes us co-creators of our reality, and places within our grasp the power to shape our destinies.

Recognizing this interconnectedness, we come to understand that by changing our internal landscape, we can influence the greater cosmos. This principle not only underscores the power of our thoughts but also the immense potential of affirmations in reprogramming the canvas of our subconscious.

Arm yourself with these affirmations, for they are your philosopher's stone. Let's embark on this quest to transmute the lead of self-doubt and fear into the gold of self-belief and courage. This is the alchemy of the mind, the great work that awaits.

Emerging from the Shadows

In the ancient alchemical texts, one is introduced to the concept of transmutation—the mystical process where base metals are transformed into gold. The journey of overcoming low self-esteem is no different than this sacred art. We begin with the leaden weight of doubt, self-deprecation, and an obscured sense of self-worth. But like the diligent alchemist, with intention and understanding, we can transmute these burdens into the golden light of self-assurance and reverence for our own being.

The caverns of our psyche hold the echoes of past experiences, voices—some our own, some from others—that might have cast shadows on our inherent radiance. These whispers, over time, bury the innate belief in our worth, shrouding it in layers of uncertainty. But every shadow implies the existence of light. The light of self-worth is always within us, waiting for the alchemical process to unveil it.

To embark on this transformative journey, we must first descend into the subterranean realms of our subconscious. With the lantern of introspection, we seek the roots of our self-doubt. Each root traced back, each moment relived and understood, becomes the philosopher's stone in our hands, a tool of great power.

The true source of self-worth isn't in external validation, accolades, or fleeting moments of recognition. It lies deep within, a timeless essence that is untouched by the ebbs and flows of life. Recognizing this is the first step in the great work we undertake—the alchemy of the self.

Drawing from the deep wells of Hermetic philosophy, Stoicism, and alchemical transformation, these affirmations are crafted to align your inner world with the cosmic dance of creation and existence. They serve as a guide to illuminate your path, helping you to transmute everyday challenges into golden opportunities and to recognize the unshakeable worth inherent within you.

As you repeat these affirmations, allow each word to resonate deeply, to echo in the chambers of your heart and mind. Visualize yourself as the master alchemist of your life, transforming leaden doubts into golden self-belief. These are not just words; they are tools for transformation, designed to fortify your inner strength and manifest a reality that reflects your highest respect and love for yourself. Let this be your alchemical ritual, a daily practice that molds self-respect and dignity into a pillar of unwavering power amidst the tempests of life.

Let's delve into the affirmations to illuminate our path from the shadows.

- I am the Philosopher's Stone; my intrinsic worth transforms all challenges into golden opportunities.

- I am an eternal flame of self-worth, unaffected by the winds of external judgment.

- I am the mirror of respect and love for myself, as my external world mirrors the respect and love I hold within.

- I am continually evolving, shedding the weight of doubt to reveal my luminous essence.

- I am the master alchemist of my destiny, forging self-belief from the crucible of past trials.

- I am empowered by Stoic truth, finding strength not in external validation, but in my unyielding inner fortitude.

- I am the universe's grand design; my worth is woven into the very fabric of existence.

- I am like the hermetic seal, keeping my self-esteem intact, preserving my inner treasures against all external pressures.

- I am drawing upon ancient wisdom with each breath, recognizing the divinity and worth in my being.

- I am a pillar of self-respect and dignity, unwavering amidst life's tempests, knowing the strength of my foundation.

- I am aligned with the Hermetic principle, understanding that the perception of my worth begins within and is reflected outward.

- I am refined through the crucible of existence; every experience adds to the purity of my gold, magnifying my self-worth.

- I am defined not by externals but by an unyielding fortress of worth from within, as taught by the Stoics.

- I am drawing from the alchemical fountains, recognizing self-doubt as merely a stage in my journey toward radiant self-belief.

- I am the external manifestation of the boundless respect I cultivate internally.

- I am guided by the wisdom of ages, recognizing that every shadow cast upon me accentuates my luminous nature.

- I am both the lead and the gold in the great dance of duality, understanding the value each provides.

- I am timeless and invaluable, a testament to the universe's grandeur and the Hermetic truth of oneness.

- I am finding my worth in stoic silence, not in external voices but in the symphony of my soul.

- I am the alchemist who sees past the veil of doubts, focusing on the eternal gem of my being.

- I am grounded in Hermetic wisdom, realizing the cosmos's vastness mirrors the boundless worth within me.

- I am an alchemist in life; every tribulation is a catalyst that refines and enhances my self-worth.

- I am welcoming life's tempests like the Stoics, knowing they polish the diamond of my esteem.

- I am an irreplaceable piece in the grand mosaic of existence, brimming with unique value.

- I am embracing every phase of my journey, knowing that even in dissolution lies the promise of rebirth and self-discovery.

- I am guided by "Know Thyself"; through introspection, I unearth the boundless treasure of my worth.

- I am like the alchemist, consciously blending my experiences to extract the elixir of self-confidence.

- I am embracing Stoic resilience, remaining unaffected by fleeting opinions and grounding my worth in timeless truths.

- I am both the creator and the creation, invaluable in every form, reminded by the Hermetic dance of creation echoing within me.

- I am shedding all that dims my light in the silent chambers of alchemical transformation, emerging with shining esteem.

- I am a seasoned alchemist, transmuting every fragment of doubt into stepping stones of self-assurance.

- I am unshaken by life's changing tides of judgment, my self-worth as firm as the Stoics' stance against the tempest.

- I am resonating with the cosmic symphony, each note affirming the irreplaceable melody of my being, grounded in Hermetic understanding.

- I am the alchemical flame refining my perceptions, illuminating the gold of my inherent worth.

- I am finding solace in stoic contemplation, knowing my essence's value remains inviolable, irrespective of external events.

- I am containing multitudes; my multifaceted being is a testament to the universe's diverse beauty and strength.

- I am embracing the alchemical principle of coagulation, forging my myriad experiences into a cohesive testament of undeniable worth.

- I am soaring above the mundane, guided by Hermetic winds, gaining perspective on my unique journey's infinite value.

- I am focusing on my intrinsic value, steady and unblinking like the Stoic's gaze, undistracted by life's mirages.

- I am remembering that in every moment of dissolution lies the potent seed of rebirth.

- I am steeped in Hermetic wisdom, grasping that my inner universe brims with stars of worth, each shining uniquely.

- I am firm in my self-worth, rooted in the unshakeable bedrock of self-awareness, unmoved by external chaos like the Stoics.

- I am revealing that even in my rawest form, my essence holds boundless value.

- I am radiating worth from an unending source within, as all emanates from the One.

- I am building the fortress of my self-esteem brick by brick, with every conscious thought and action.

- I am reminded of my cosmic significance, the universe mirroring back the immeasurable worth I hold in its reflection.

- I am invigorated by the realization of my worth, like the alchemist's elixir, bestowing vitality and purpose.

- I am seeing that true self-worth is anchored in eternal truths, not influenced by the fleeting.

- I am a reservoir of infinite value, and every moment of my life reaffirms the unshakable belief in my own worth.

- I am emerging time and again with a purer, brighter, and unwavering self-esteem, embraced by the transformative fire of alchemy.

The Embrace of the Self

In the hallowed annals of alchemical lore, one encounters the legendary Philosopher's Stone—a substance said to possess the power to transform base metals into gold and grant eternal life. In the spiritual fabric of our existence, self-love is our own personal Philosopher's Stone. It possesses the wondrous ability to transmute the basest of doubts and fears into the most radiant expressions of love and acceptance. It is the elixir that grants us not physical immortality, but an enduring embrace of our essence through the fluctuations of life.

The journey towards genuine self-love is akin to the alchemist's quest, fraught with trials and tests, but also illuminated by profound revelations. In the crucible of our experiences, we often encounter elements of self-rejection, criticism, and neglect. Yet, like the masterful alchemist, with the right intent and understanding, we have the power to transform these elements, creating a potent potion of love and compassion for our own being.

The Hermetic teachings whisper of the principle "As within, so without." This profound truth underscores the significance of self-love. For the world we perceive without is but a reflection of the inner realm. By nurturing a deep and genuine love for oneself, we subtly shift the universe within, and in doing so, reshape the universe without.

It is an endeavor worthy of the greatest alchemists—for to master self-love is to touch upon the divine. It is the great work, the magnum opus of our inner alchemy. As we traverse this chapter, let each word be a guiding star, leading us closer to the sanctum where our true self awaits, ready to be embraced with all the love and reverence it rightfully deserves. And as we merge with this self, we become the gold sought by alchemists of old, a being of inestimable worth and luminous love.

Let's explore the affirmations from The Embrace of the Self, focusing on cultivating self-love.

- I am like the Philosopher's Stone; my love for myself transforms every experience, revealing the golden essence beneath.

- I nurture an unwavering flame of self-love in silence, shining brilliantly amidst life's trials and tribulations.

- I am the reflection of the love I cultivate within, creating a world filled with compassion and understanding.

- I recognize self-love as the ultimate elixir through the alchemical process, rejuvenating my spirit and fortifying my heart.

- With each heartbeat, I am reminded of the Hermetic truth: I am a universe unto myself, deserving of boundless love.

- I understand that self-love is a fortress, protecting me from the storms of external judgments.

- I am an alchemist transforming every doubt into a reaffirmation of my worth and self-love.

- The dance of duality teaches me to embrace both light and shadow within, cherishing every facet of my being.

- I find that true self-love is rooted not in fleeting feelings but in the eternal embrace of my essence.

- I see that the journey to self-love is a continuous cycle of dissolution and coagulation, breaking down only to rebuild stronger and more radiant.

- In the reflective pool of teachings, I see that loving oneself is the first ripple that transforms the entirety of the cosmic ocean.

- My self-love remains steadfast, irrespective of the world's ever-shifting perceptions.

- With discerning gaze, I recognize that self-love is the crucible where my essence is continuously purified and renewed.

- Just as the cosmos pulses with boundless love and potential, so does the universe within me.

- I understand that true self-love does not seek validation but is anchored in the unchanging truth of my worth.

- I cherish each moment of introspection, for it adds another layer to the rich fabric of my self-love.

- The winds whisper the age-old secret: To love oneself is to unlock the doors to infinite realms of possibility and magic.

- I look deeply within, finding a reservoir of love that never depletes but constantly replenishes.

- In the laboratory of life, every experience, whether bitter or sweet, contributes to the perfect potion of self-love.

- I am reminded that the grand dance of the universe is also enacted within me, deserving of awe and deep reverence.

- I realize that self-love is an inner sanctuary, impervious to the winds of external critique and fleeting judgments.

- I see potential in all; likewise, every facet of my being holds a promise, awaiting the tender embrace of love.

- "As the All mirrors the One," the boundless love of the cosmos is but a reflection of the love I hold for myself.

- I unearth the timeless wisdom that to love oneself is the truest form of reverence to the universe.

- Past hurts and regrets become fertile ground, nurturing seeds of profound self-love through transmutation.

- The balance between the macrocosm and microcosm reminds me that the love that steers the stars also courses through my veins.

- I discern that the truest form of love is self-generated, its source ever-flowing from within.

- I harmonize every shade of my being, creating a symphony of self-love and acceptance.

- I listen to the heartbeat of the universe in silence, and it echoes back a song of love for the unique melody I bring.

- I understand that self-love isn't an end but a journey, evolving and deepening with every step.

- In steadfast gaze upon truth, I see that my worth is not defined by others but acknowledged and cherished from within.

- I know that in every substance lies a hidden gem; similarly, beneath layers of self-doubt, my radiant self-love awaits discovery.

- "The All vibrates," so does the rhythm of my heart resonate with unwavering love for the soul it sustains.

- I embrace the impermanence of life, cherishing the eternal flame of self-love that burns steadily within.

- Every moment of vulnerability is transformed into a testament of my unyielding love and acceptance through alchemical processes.

- In embracing both my strengths and flaws, I find the perfect equilibrium of self-love.

- My love for myself stands tall and unshaken, its foundation deeply rooted in truth, remaining unmoved in the storm.

- I mold and shape my self-perception, crafting a statue that radiates self-love from every angle with patient hand.

- I understand that in the dance of duality, my love for myself is both the dance and the dancer, eternally intertwined.

- I fathom that self-love is not mere sentiment but a profound understanding and acceptance of my ever-evolving self.

- I declare that self-love is the compass by which I navigate the vast seas of existence, with a sense of purpose.

- In every endeavor, there lies faith in transformation; in my heart, I hold faith that self-love is the golden key unlocking my true potential.

- As teachings illuminate the unity of all, I recognize that in loving myself, I am harmonizing with the universal symphony of love.

- Even in solitude, I am in the comforting embrace of self-love, a companion ever loyal and true.

- I choose to see and celebrate the unique beauty in every aspect of my being, finding beauty in every element.

- I realize that my journey of self-love is a reflection of the cosmos' eternal dance of unity and distinction.

- I cherish my self-love as the most genuine testament to my existence, with unwavering commitment to truth.

- I continuously refine my understanding and expression of self-love, letting it shine brighter with each day.

- The wisdom of "As above, so below" whispers that the love that governs the vast cosmos also nurtures and sustains my innermost being.

- I hold that self-love is not a mere feeling but a profound choice, one I commit to with every breath.

Unshakable Pillars

In the ancient and secretive chambers of alchemists, the transmutation of base metals into gold was not merely a physical endeavor but a symbol of spiritual and psychological transformation. As with these ancient practices, our journey to build unyielding confidence is both profound and mysterious, an inner alchemy of mind and soul.

The alchemical crucible is a vessel of change, wherein substances are melded, dissolved, and reborn in purer forms. Similarly, our inner world is a crucible, where doubts, fears, and insecurities can be transformed, giving birth to the golden aura of unwavering confidence. True confidence, much like the Philosopher's Stone sought by alchemists of old, is not a fleeting possession to be acquired but an innate quality to be realized and refined.

The Hermetic principles teach of the intricate dance between the macrocosm and microcosm, reminding us that the same forces shaping the universe are at work within us. In this cosmic dance, confidence is our innate harmony with the universe, an affirmation of our rightful place in the vast fabric of existence.

Just as an alchemist relies on ancient wisdom and inner intuition to guide their transformations, so must we turn inward, drawing from the deep wells of our experiences and innate wisdom to forge the pillars of our confidence. These pillars, once established, stand resolute against the tempests of doubt, casting a shadow that is the very embodiment of our true potential.

This chapter beckons you into the alchemical laboratory of your psyche. Here, amidst the arcane symbols and bubbling elixirs, lies the great work of crafting unshakable confidence. It is a journey not of external validation but of internal realization, of recognizing and harnessing the powerful elixir of self-belief that has always resided within you.

Let's dive into the affirmations from the chapter, Unshakable Pillars.

- Like the Stoic, unperturbed by the raging storm, I stand firm in my convictions, my confidence unyielding and true.

- In the Alchemist's crucible, substances transform; likewise, every experience molds my confidence, making it more resplendent.

- As the Hermetic teachings emphasize the unity of all, I recognize that my confidence is an echo of the universe's unwavering trust in me.

- Drawing from Stoic resolve, I understand that confidence is not mere bravado, but a deep knowing of one's place in the grand fabric of existence.

- With the Alchemist's faith in transformation, I see challenges not as obstacles but as catalysts, refining and bolstering my confidence.

- Heeding the Hermetic principle of correspondence, "As above, so below," the confidence that governs the stars also fortifies my spirit.

- Inspired by Stoic clarity, I realize that true confidence springs not from external applause but from the harmonious chorus of my inner truths.

- As the Alchemist distills essence from matter, I distill confidence from every victory and lesson, forging a shield of self-belief.

- In the Hermetic dance of energies, I embrace that my confidence is both the rhythm and the response, a perpetual dance of self-assuredness.

- Guided by Stoic wisdom, I stand tall, knowing that my confidence is a testament to my journey, a beacon illuminating my path.

- Embracing Stoic fortitude, I find strength not in the absence of doubt, but in my ability to rise above it, my confidence shining brighter.

- The Alchemist understands the secret of turning lead into gold; in the same vein, I transform my insecurities into unwavering confidence.

- As Hermetic wisdom reveals the interconnectedness of all things, I draw confidence from the universe's endless dance, feeling deeply in tune with its rhythm.

- Grounded in Stoic perspective, I see setbacks not as failures but as stepping stones, each one building my confidence higher and stronger.

- As the Alchemist melds disparate elements into a harmonious whole, I blend my strengths and weaknesses, forging an unbreakable alloy of confidence.

- Through Hermetic eyes, I perceive the mirroring of the inner and outer worlds; the boundless confidence of the cosmos is reflected within my very soul.

- With Stoic simplicity, I strip away the extraneous, understanding that genuine confidence is unadorned, standing tall in its authentic glory.

- Emulating the Alchemist's patience, I cultivate my confidence over time, knowing each moment adds a layer to its brilliant sheen.

- Absorbing the Hermetic principle of vibration, I attune myself to the frequency of confidence, resonating with its powerful energy.

- Inspired by Stoic introspection, I realize that true confidence is not shouted from rooftops but whispered in the quiet assurance of one's heart.

- Channeling Stoic resilience, I affirm that my confidence is not transient but remains steady, weathering life's ebb and flow.

- The Alchemist perceives the potential in every substance; similarly, within every doubt, I see an opportunity to solidify my confidence.

- Echoing the Hermetic axiom, "All is mind," I understand that the realm of confidence is mental, and by mastering my thoughts, I master my confidence.

- Embodying Stoic independence, I root my confidence not in others' perceptions but in my unwavering self-awareness and understanding.

- Through the Alchemist's lens, each day is an elixir; imbibing its lessons and joys, I fortify the potion of my burgeoning confidence.

- Inspired by Hermetic balance, I harmonize both my achievements and missteps, recognizing that each contributes to my holistic confidence.

- With Stoic wisdom, I acknowledge that confidence is not the absence of vulnerability but the courage to embrace it.

- In the Alchemist's pursuit of perfection, I continuously refine my essence, distilling a purer, more profound confidence from life's experiences.

- Drawing from Hermetic teachings, I recognize the dual nature of all things and thus find confidence both in action and stillness.

- Grounded in Stoic reflections, I find that my deepest wellspring of confidence arises not from what I do but from who I truly am.

- Guided by Stoic humility, I comprehend that genuine confidence is rooted in understanding my worth without diminishing that of others.

- The Alchemist, in their wisdom, finds magic in the mundane; I too see every moment as a chance to nurture and expand my reservoir of confidence.

- As the Hermetic doctrine elucidates the principle of rhythm, I too dance with life, my confidence undeterred by its highs and lows.

- Through Stoic lenses, I discern that confidence isn't about always being right but having the courage to admit when I'm wrong and grow from it.

- With the Alchemist's heart, I cherish every experience, understanding that both trials and triumphs are ingredients in the crucible of my evolving confidence.

- Reflecting upon Hermetic insights, I grasp that as the universe expands, so does the potential of my inner confidence, limitless and boundless.

- Anchored in Stoic tenets, I remind myself that confidence does not shout but is the quiet, steady voice that says, "I can, and I will."

- Embracing the Alchemist's trust in transformation, I acknowledge past insecurities, using them as catalysts to crystallize my present confidence.

- Drawing from the Hermetic understanding of polarity, I harness both my strengths and weaknesses, forging a balanced and unwavering confidence.

- Inspired by Stoic reflections, I understand that true confidence is the peaceful intersection of knowing oneself and being at peace with what one discovers.

- Through Stoic discernment, I recognize that the fountain of my confidence is not fed by external praise but springs from the depths of self-knowledge.

- In the spirit of the Alchemist, I embrace every challenge, knowing that in the furnace of adversity, the purest gold of confidence is forged.

- In line with the Hermetic principle of causation, I realize that every thought and action ripples outward, and so I choose those that fortify my confidence.

- Guided by Stoic endurance, I stand unyielding in the face of doubt, allowing my confidence to be the rock upon which life's waves crash.

- With the Alchemist's unrelenting faith, I recognize that the elixir of confidence is concocted not just in moments of triumph, but also in the depths of despair.

- Heeding Hermetic wisdom, I understand that the cosmos pulsates with boundless confidence, and I am but a reflection of that celestial magnificence.

- With Stoic introspection, I cultivate confidence not as an armor against the world, but as a bridge connecting me to the essence of all things.

- Embodying the Alchemist's reverence for metamorphosis, I allow life's trials to shape and mold me, emerging with a radiant and unbreakable confidence.

- Reflecting on the Hermetic law of gender, I nurture both the masculine and feminine aspects of my confidence, achieving a harmonious inner unity.

- Grounded in Stoic simplicity, I find solace in authenticity, understanding that my truest confidence shines when I am unabashedly myself.

Walking Through Fire

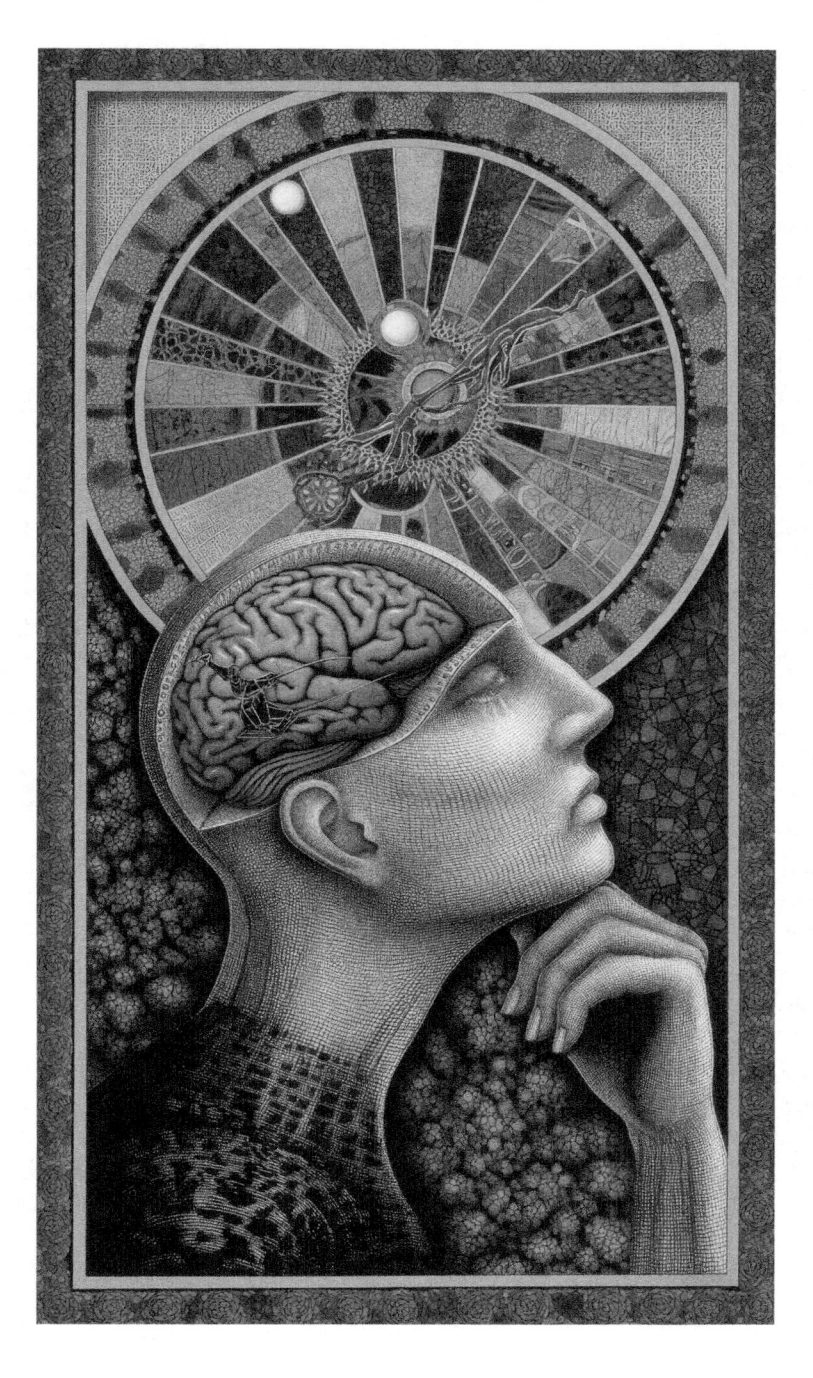

In the twilight corridors of the human soul, there resides a force as ancient as the universe itself — fear. Like a shadow cast by the duality of our existence, it hovers, sometimes quiet, other times overwhelmingly loud. From the early myths told around campfires to the timeless tales of Joseph Campbell, fear has been the dragon guarding the entrance to the cave of our potential.

Every hero in myth, every individual on the journey of life, encounters this fire-breathing beast. And just as the alchemist believes that within the crucible, base metals transform into gold, so too does the fire of our fears hold the potential for our most profound transformation. For fear is not just a sentinel barring us from our destiny, it is also a guide, pointing the way to the very challenges we need to face for our evolution.

Joseph Campbell's elucidation of the Hero's Journey reminds us that confronting and overcoming our deepest fears is an essential rite of passage. It is in the belly of the whale, in the dark heart of the labyrinth, that we discover our hidden strengths and retrieve the treasures of our true self. The descent into the underworld, a motif found in countless myths, mirrors our own journey into the recesses of our psyche, where fear holds court.

But, like the alchemist's Magnum Opus, confronting this fear is the great work that we must all undertake. To walk through fire, to dare to face the dragon and retrieve the gold of our true essence, is the path of transformation. As we confront and understand our fears, we become the alchemical magicians of our own lives, transmuting paralyzing terror into empowering courage, converting the shackles that bind us into the wings that let us soar.

To truly understand and confront fear is not just to overcome an obstacle but to realize a deeper aspect of oneself. It is to acknowledge the trials and tribulations as necessary elements of the Hero's Journey, understanding that every challenge faced, every fear confronted, is a step closer to the self-realization and mastery that awaits.

As we venture forth in this chapter, may you find the courage to face the dragon, to embrace the fire, and emerge not just unscathed but reborn — stronger, wiser, and ever more luminous. For in the alchemical union of courage and understanding, the grip of fear is loosened, and we find our true freedom.

Let's delve into the affirmations from the chapter, Walking Through Fire.

- I am the hero of my own journey, boldly facing every challenge, understanding that each fear faced is a threshold crossed on my path to wholeness.

- I am a vessel of transformation, turning the challenges of my fears into the gold of courage and resilience, refining with each trial.

- I am rooted in ancient wisdom, embracing every moment as an opportunity to grow, recognizing that fear is but a fleeting impression.

- I am in harmony with the universal principle of polarity, seeing that fear has its opposite in love and choosing to align myself with the latter.

- I am on a timeless quest, and like the heroes of old, I understand that the dragons of fear guard the deepest treasures of my soul.

- I embody the spirit of transformation, using life's experiences to shift fear into insight, bravery, and newfound strength.

- I am fortified by enduring tenets, viewing adversities not as setbacks but as lessons, knowing that external events do not disturb me, only my perceptions do.

- I am attuned to the ancient wisdom that the mind is a powerful tool; thus, I hold dominion over my fears by mastering my thoughts and emotions.

- I am a traveler on a profound journey, and with every fear faced and conquered, I return enriched and enlightened to my inner sanctum.

- I am an eternal learner in the tradition of introspection and self-mastery, recognizing that amidst life's challenges, the essence of my being shines brightly, undimmed by fear.

- I am a beacon of inner strength, undeterred by the specters of doubt, for I know they are mere phantoms passing in the night.

- I am anchored in timeless truths, drawing strength from the wellspring of lessons past, facing fear as a challenge to be overcome.

- I am the master of my destiny, weaving my journey of life with threads of courage, determination, and hope, even in the face of adversity.

- I am the keeper of my inner flame, and though the winds of fear may blow, they cannot extinguish the fiery core of my resolve.

- I am guided by the compass of inner wisdom, always pointing me towards growth, understanding that the shadows of fear only deepen in the absence of light.

- I am a warrior of spirit, clad in the armor of self-belief, wielding the sword of knowledge, and using it to cut through the chains of fear.

- I am the sculptor of my soul, chiseling away the unnecessary, revealing the masterpiece hidden beneath layers of apprehension.

- I am rooted in the profound rhythm of the universe, syncing my heartbeat with its timeless dance, realizing that fear is but a fleeting beat in the grand symphony of existence.

- I am a seeker of hidden treasures, knowing that they often lie behind daunting challenges, and I embrace them, for overcoming fear is the key to unveiling these gems.

- I am the alchemist of my emotions, skillfully turning the heavy lead of fear into the radiant gold of confidence and self-assuredness.

- I am the captain of my soul's voyage, navigating through storms of fear with a compass of inner strength and unwavering focus.

- I am a soul woven of resilience and determination, where threads of fear once added darkness, now contribute to the contrast that defines my growth.

- I am a sanctuary of calm, even when surrounded by the tempests of apprehension, for I know that after every storm, the skies clear.

- I am the guardian of my inner sanctum, admitting only thoughts that uplift and empower, leaving fears at the door as unwelcome guests.

- I am a river that flows unwaveringly towards its destiny, knowing that occasional rapids of fear only add vigor to my journey.

- I am the maestro of my life's symphony, and while some notes of fear might be sharp, they add depth to the music of my existence.

- I am grounded in the soil of ancient wisdom, drawing nourishment for my growth and using the rocks of fear as stepping stones.

- I am the torchbearer in the cave of uncertainty, using the flame of my willpower to illuminate the path and keep the shadows of doubt at bay.

- I am a mighty oak, and though the winds of fear may rustle my leaves, they cannot uproot my steadfast spirit.

- I am the scribe of my life's narrative, choosing to pen chapters of triumph and growth, making fear a mere footnote.

- I am a phoenix, ever-rising, and even if fear attempts to turn me to ash, it only sets the stage for my next luminous ascent.

- I am the silent observer within, watching the ebb and flow of emotions, knowing that fear is but a transient wave in the vast ocean of consciousness.

- I am a fortress of determination, where the winds of anxiety may batter my walls, but they stand unyielding and unbroken.

- I am the moon, shedding light in the darkest of nights, showing that even in moments of deep fear, there is a guiding luminance within.

- I am the keeper of ancient echoes, drawing from timeless wisdom to speak to my fears, reminding them of their insignificance in the grand fabric of existence.

- I am the bridge spanning the chasm of doubt, built brick by brick with my experiences, ensuring that fear remains beneath and never becomes my path.

- I am the lens that chooses its focus, zooming in on aspirations and dreams, rendering the fears blurry and distant.

- I am the silent desert, where fears are but mirages, fleeting and illusory, dissolving under the relentless sun of my awareness.

- I am the gardener of my mind, tending to thoughts that bloom into beautiful realities, pulling out the weeds of fear before they take root.

- I am the gatekeeper at the temple of my spirit, granting entry only to those beliefs that resonate with growth and positivity, while turning away the specters of fear.

- I am the alchemist of my soul, seeing fear not as a foe but as raw material, awaiting the transformative touch of understanding.

- I am the mountain peak, standing tall amidst storm clouds of doubt, knowing that above me lies the eternal clarity of purpose and below, the valley of past fears overcome.

- I am the harmonizer of my inner symphony, blending the minor chords of fear into a song of resilience, determination, and victory.

- I am the explorer of inner realms, charting courses through seas of uncertainty, confident in the stars of my higher understanding guiding me.

- I am the flame that dances, not deterred by gusts of worry, for every sway and shift tells a tale of resilience and adaptability.

- I am the hourglass, patient and enduring, as fears like sands slip through, transient and destined to pass.

- I am the sovereign of my destiny, donning the crown of courage and holding the scepter of wisdom, ruling over the lands of fear with grace and foresight.

- I am the story's hero, for every shadow I confront becomes a chapter of growth, a testament to the strength found in facing fears.

- I am the weaver of dreams, intertwining threads of hope, ambition, and courage, rendering fears mere strands lost in a vibrant fabric.

- I am the dawn after the darkest night, a reminder that no matter the depth of fear, the promise of a new day and renewed hope always lies ahead.

Mastering the Inner Realm

In the vast cosmos of existence, among the celestial bodies and infinite stars, there exists a realm equally profound, yet it lies not outside, but within. The inner world, our mind's universe, is where the dance of thoughts, desires, and emotions takes place. Here, where dreams take shape and fears lurk in shadows, lies the ultimate realm of control: the self.

Friedrich Nietzsche once mused,

"He who has a why to live can bear almost any how."

These words hint at the autonomy we possess, the sheer power of purpose and choice. It is here, in recognizing our ability to choose, that we tap into an ancient well of control, shaping our inner landscapes as the alchemist melds and transmutes base metals into gold. To master oneself is perhaps the most intricate alchemical process of all. For within the crucible of the mind, the raw elements of impulse, desire, and instinct can be transformed into the refined gold of willpower, intent, and discernment.

This mastery is not about suppression, but understanding; not about dominance, but alignment. It's about harnessing the currents of the inner realm to sail purposefully, rather than being tossed about by life's tempestuous seas. True autonomy emerges not from external freedoms, but from the deep acknowledgment and exercise of our power of choice within.

In this journey of introspection, we'll discover that the chains we once felt binding us are often self-forged, but so too is the key to our liberation. By turning our gaze inward and daring to confront the chaos, we embrace the potential to shape and mold our destiny. Like the alchemist, we endeavor to transmute, refine, and elevate our essence. It is the great work of our time, a task both demanding and rewarding, where we transcend the given and venture into the realm of the possible, forever in pursuit of our own Übermensch, our higher self.

Dive deep into this chapter, and let us explore the corridors of choice, autonomy, and control. Let it be a beacon guiding you towards mastering the inner realm, towards a future shaped by intent and crowned with the laurel of self-mastery.

Let's dive into the affirmations from the chapter, Mastering the Inner Realm.

- I am the master of my fate, shaping my inner realm with the fire of will and the hammer of intent.

- I am the dance and the dancer, moving in rhythm with life's challenges and orchestrating my own destiny.

- I am the alchemist of my soul, constantly transmuting doubt into determination and apathy into passion.

- I am the silent observer, watching the play of desires and impulses, ever poised to choose my course with wisdom.

- I am the sovereign of my thoughts, reigning over the vast empire of the mind, where chaos bends to the order of my decree.

- I am the sculptor of my character, and with every chisel stroke, I shape the marble of potential into a masterpiece of purpose.

- I am the keeper of my own flame, ensuring it never wanes but always burns with the brilliance of self-awareness.

- I am the guardian at the gateways of perception, sifting through external influences and retaining only what resonates with my higher purpose.

- I am the philosopher of my existence, questioning, pondering, and forever seeking the truth that lies hidden within.

- I am the hermit and the emperor, for while I seek wisdom in solitude, I exercise control and mastery in the world's bustling theater.

- I am the architect of my beliefs, laying each brick with care and crafting the sanctuary of my convictions.

- I am the captain of my inner voyage, steering through the tempests of doubt with the compass of self-assuredness.

- I am the gold refined in the crucible of life's trials, emerging purer, stronger, and more radiant with every challenge faced.

- I am the unwavering pillar amidst life's quakes, rooted in self-understanding and crowned with the knowledge of my own worth.

- I am the seeker on life's labyrinthine path, finding meaning in each twist and turn, every setback, and stride forward.

- I am the master of my emotions, neither suppressing nor indulging, but observing and understanding their ebb and flow.

- I am the artist of my narrative, painting my story with strokes of intentionality and shades of self-respect.

- I am the warrior of my battles, armed with resilience, shielded by purpose, and driven by an unwavering spirit.

- I am the bridge between thought and action, ensuring that my deeds resonate with the harmonies of my deepest truths.

- I am the gatekeeper of my energy, channeling it towards endeavors that elevate, inspire, and resonate with my higher calling.

- I am the torchbearer in the caverns of uncertainty, lighting up the pathways with my innate wisdom and insight.

- I am the fountainhead of my aspirations, continuously renewing my passion and quenching my thirst for progress.

- I am the oak in the forest of fleeting thoughts, grounded in my convictions and reaching skyward with ambition.

- I am the chalice capturing the essence of experiences, savoring the nectar and discarding the dross.

- I am the keeper of the equilibrium, balancing the scales of desire and contentment, passion and peace.

- I am the sentinel at the dawn of my decisions, heralding choices that align with the symphony of my soul's purpose.

- I am the scribe of my own epic, chronicling tales of tenacity, chapters of courage, and verses of victory.

- I am the magnet drawing experiences that refine and define, attract and act upon my higher purpose.

- I am the prism refracting life's experiences, casting a spectrum of lessons learned and wisdom won.

- I am the timeless essence, unswayed by fleeting moments, ever-present in the eternal now.

- I am the forge where willpower and desire meld, fashioning a weapon of unwavering determination.

- I am the cosmic dance of duality, harmonizing the push and pull of life with grace and poise.

- I am the gardener of my soul's soil, nurturing seeds of potential and weeding out doubts that hinder growth.

- I am the mirror reflecting clarity, seeing beyond the surface to recognize the boundless depths of my essence.

- I am the alchemical vessel, transforming base impulses into refined actions through introspection and intention.

- I am the maestro of my life's orchestra, ensuring every instrument, every note, aligns with the music of my making.

- I am the watchtower on the frontier of consciousness, vigilant against limiting beliefs, always inviting expansive thought.

- I am the poet of my existence, finding rhythm in chaos, beauty in adversity, and meaning in the mundane.

- I am the sailor charting courses unknown, embracing the winds of change, and navigating with unwavering focus.

- I am the guardian of the sacred flame within, ensuring it never dims, always illuminating my path and purpose.

- I am the wellspring of resilience, rising with renewed vigor, no matter the weight of life's burdens.

- I am the enigma that solves itself, delving into life's mysteries with curiosity and emerging with understanding.

- I am the chrysalis and the butterfly, ever-evolving, transitioning from phases of introspection to expansive expression.

- I am the lighthouse amidst storms, standing tall, emitting a beacon of hope and guidance for both myself and others.

- I am the cartographer of my inner landscapes, mapping terrains of emotion, intellect, and intuition.

- I am the master potter, molding my character with skilled hands, shaping my essence with intentionality and vision.

- I am the wanderer and the destination, on a journey to self, discovering treasures within every step of the way.

- I am the custodian of my legacy, writing a saga of empowerment, evolution, and enduring grace.

- I am the echo in the canyon of existence, resonating with truths timeless, and virtues virtuous.

- I am the key and the lock, holding the power to unlock potentials untapped, and doors unexplored.

The Fortress Within

In the vast landscape of existence, the mind is both the battleground and the sanctum. A place where thoughts clash, emotions wage wars, and yet, amidst all this turmoil, resides an invincible fortress. It is this fortress that the alchemists speak of, not one built with stone and mortar, but one forged from experience, wisdom, and unyielding resilience.

As we traverse the path of life, we are often faced with tempests that challenge the integrity of our inner fortress. These tempests, in their varying intensities, come not to weaken us, but to test the strength of our mental ramparts. Like gold purified in fire, the mind, when faced with adversity, has the potential to emerge stronger, more luminous, and unyielding.

Marcus Aurelius, the philosopher king, amidst the complexities of ruling an empire and the challenges of war, found solace in the fortress of his mind. For him, the outer world was but a reflection of the inner. As Marcus Aurelius wisely articulated,

> "You have power over your mind – not outside events. Realize this, and you will find strength."

It is in this realization that the great work of alchemy begins, a transformation from vulnerability to invincibility, from flux to fortitude.

Within these pages, we shall delve deep into the catacombs of the psyche, uncovering the tools, techniques, and tales that have, for eons, aided sages and seekers in the fortification of their mental domain. Remember, the strength of the fortress is not just in its walls, but in the guardian who watches over it. Become that guardian, realize the alchemical power within, and witness the transformation of every challenge into an opportunity, every adversity into an ally.

This, dear reader, is your invitation to the sacred art of cultivating mental strength, to understand, nurture, and ultimately, unveil the impregnable fortress within.

Let's journey through the affirmations from the chapter, The Fortress Within.

- I am the master of my inner domain, turning chaos into order, through reflection and intention.

- I am the sage within, drawing from the infinite wellspring of wisdom, rooted in experiences and insights.

- I am the alchemist of my psyche, transforming every adversity into an ally, every challenge into a stepping stone.

- I am unyielding like the mountain, standing tall and firm, no matter how fierce the winds of life blow.

- I am the philosopher of my existence, observing the play of fate, yet knowing the power of free will.

- I am the strategist, foreseeing the ebbs and flows of life, always poised, always prepared.

- I am the keeper of the eternal flame, lighting up the corridors of my mind, dispelling shadows of doubt.

- I am the guardian of harmony, maintaining balance, embracing both light and shadow, joy and sorrow.

- I am the chalice, filled with the elixir of resilience, sipped daily to rejuvenate spirit and strengthen resolve.

- I am the fabric of life's lessons, woven with threads of courage, patience, and unceasing growth.

- I am the master sculptor, chiseling my soul to perfection with each experience life presents.

- I am the watchful sentinel, keenly observing life's patterns, learning, and evolving with each moment.

- I am the bearer of inner serenity, even when tempests rage outside, my core remains undisturbed.

- I am the navigator of my destiny, adjusting my sails as winds change, but always charting my course.

- I am the crucible, enduring the fires of trial, only to emerge purer, brighter, and stronger.

- I am the seeker of wisdom, understanding that every challenge holds a lesson, every setback a revelation.

- I am the reservoir of willpower, tapping into my inexhaustible source of determination when faced with adversity.

- I am the weaver of dreams and reality, seamlessly integrating my aspirations with actionable intent.

- I am the embodiment of patience, knowing that time reveals all truths and heals all wounds.

- I am the fortress of tenacity, standing firm in my beliefs and values, unswayed by external forces.

- I am the curator of my thoughts, selecting only those that empower and uplift.

- I am the commander of my emotions, channeling them to serve my higher purpose and growth.

- I am the silent observer, discerning transient trials from eternal truths.

- I am the resilient oak, bending but not breaking, always reaching for the sun.

- I am the wise sage, understanding that every external battle first begins within the mind.

- I am the torchbearer, illuminating the path of persistence, even in the darkest hours.

- I am the embodiment of inner peace, maintaining my center in the whirlwind of existence.

- I am the unyielding force, facing life's adversities with an unwavering spirit.

- I am the reflective pool, mirroring the lessons of life, absorbing wisdom from each reflection.

- I am the ever-evolving being, embracing growth and transformation as the essence of existence.

- I am the enduring foundation, built upon self-belief and cemented with perseverance.

- I am the cosmic dance, harmonizing with the rhythm of existence, and flourishing amidst its challenges.

- I am the alchemical gold, refined by life's trials, and radiating my intrinsic worth.

- I am the echo of ancient wisdom, resonating with the timeless virtues of courage and resilience.

- I am the vigilant guardian, preserving the sanctity of my thoughts against transient storms of doubt.

- I am the stoic mountain, unaffected by fleeting seasons, standing tall in my purpose and resolve.

- I am the boundless sky, limitless in my potential and infinite in my aspirations.

- I am the river's flow, navigating obstacles with grace, and moving with an unwavering sense of direction.

- I am the patient gardener, nurturing my growth with love and care, knowing that every season has its purpose.

- I am the beacon of hope, always radiating optimism and drawing strength from the depths of my spirit.

- I am the sovereign of my psyche, ruling with both compassion and conviction over my inner realm.

- I am the bridge between thought and action, harmoniously connecting intention with manifestation.

- I am the mosaic of experiences, each piece adding depth, color, and uniqueness to my being.

- I am the unwavering flame, burning steadily amidst life's gusts, and illuminating my path forward.

- I am the harmonious chord, resonating with balance and inner congruence, even amidst external dissonance.

- I am the sage's whisper, internalizing lessons of the past to pave a brighter tomorrow.

- I am the timeless traveler, understanding that every step, every stumble, shapes my journey's tale.

- I am the fortress of integrity, standing firm in my values, and honoring my authentic self.

- I am the resilient rose, blooming brilliantly amidst thorns, celebrating both my beauty and my strength.

- I am the eternal student, cherishing knowledge, seeking wisdom, and ever eager to evolve.

The River of Feelings

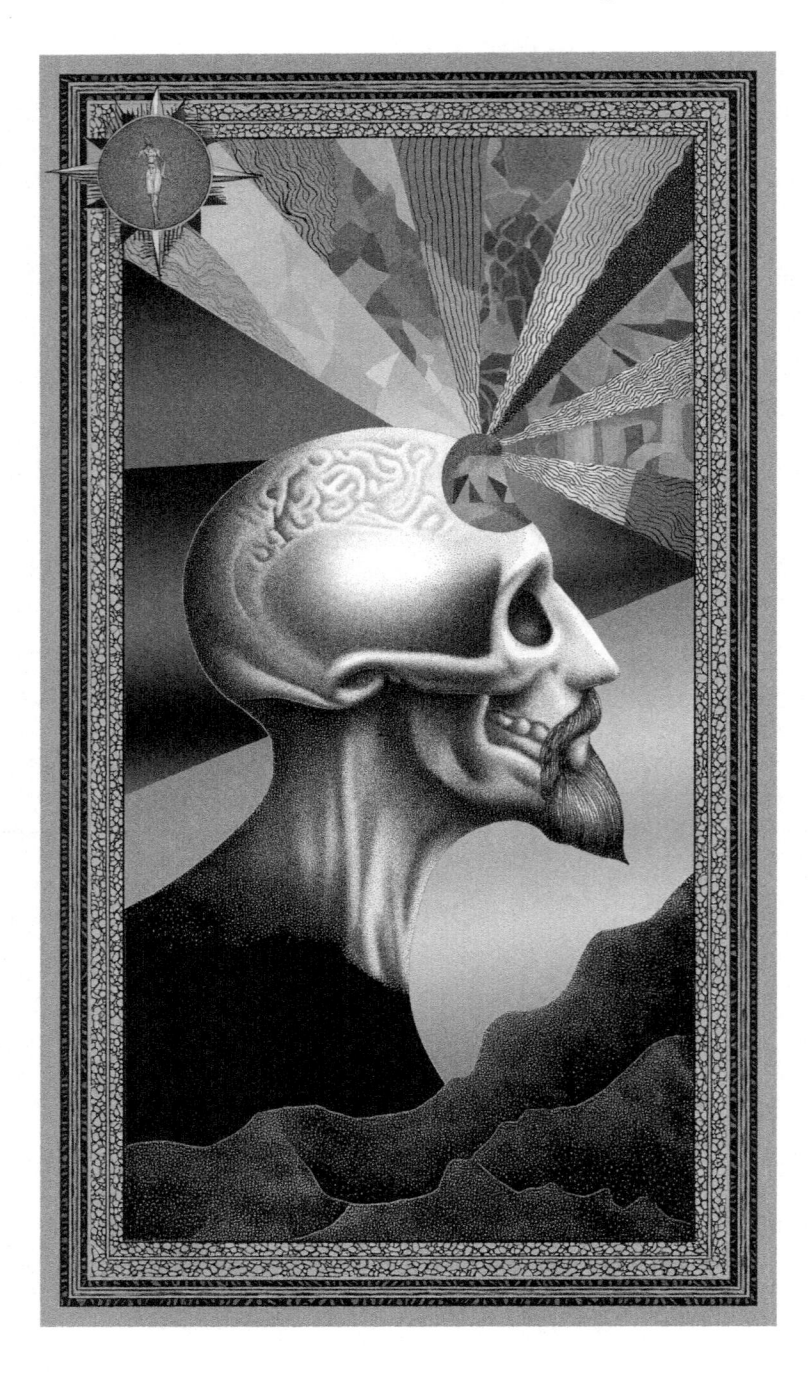

Within the heart of every human lies a vast river, one that carries the currents of joy, sorrow, anger, and love. This river, winding and meandering, is as ancient as time itself. It flows with emotions, each droplet a testament to our human experience. Like a river, our feelings possess the dual nature of serenity and storm. There are moments when the waters are placid, reflecting the tranquil azure of the skies. Then there are times when tempestuous torrents rage, muddying the clarity we once had.

Yet, as the teachings of alchemy emphasize the transformation of the base into the sublime, so too must we understand the alchemical nature of our emotions. For they are not burdens to bear, but rather raw materials awaiting refinement. They are opportunities to understand the deeper mysteries of the self, to recognize the impermanence of our experiences, and to tap into an inner alchemical process that can transmute pain into wisdom, and fear into love.

Drawing inspiration from the profound insights of Alan Watts, we are reminded of the cosmic dance of life, where every emotion, every feeling is but a note in the grand symphony of existence. There's a certain liberation in understanding that our emotions, intense as they may feel, are fleeting. They come, and they go, much like waves upon a shore. To grasp onto them, to define ourselves by them, is akin to trying to clutch water in our hands — it simply slips through, leaving us with nothing but wet palms.

But what if, instead of being at the mercy of this river, we learn to navigate its waters? What if we recognize that we are not the river, but the observer, the consciousness that witnesses its flow? In doing so, we refuse to let our lower ego, with its fleeting emotions and transient desires, overshadow our higher self — a self that is eternal, unchanging, and infinitely wise.

By embracing the teachings of both alchemy and the Eastern philosophies echoed by Alan Watts, we learn to dance with our emotions, neither repressing them nor being consumed by them. Instead, we honor their presence, learn from their wisdom, and then let them flow, understanding that, like everything in this universe, they too shall pass.

In this chapter, we embark on a mystical journey, one that will teach us the art of emotional alchemy. For within the chaos of our feelings lies a hidden order, a cosmic rhythm waiting to be discovered. Dive deep, dear reader, for the treasures of the subconscious await.

Let's navigate the affirmations found in the chapter, The River of Feelings.

- I am the silent observer, watching the dance of emotions without being entangled in them.

- I am anchored in the eternal present, where emotions flow like water, neither lingering nor stagnating.

- I am resilient, understanding that feelings are transient waves upon the vast ocean of consciousness.

- I am the alchemist of my own psyche, skillfully transmuting pain into profound wisdom.

- I am not defined by fleeting emotions, but by the timeless essence that witnesses them.

- I am in harmonious alignment with the cosmic rhythm, allowing feelings to arise, play their part, and gracefully fade.

- I am the master of my inner realm, navigating emotional turbulence with grace and understanding.

- I am grounded in the knowledge that emotions, like all things, have their season and will pass.

- I am connected to the universe's infinite dance, embracing each emotion as a note in the grand symphony of existence.

- I am unshaken, knowing that beneath the ebb and flow of feelings lies an unchanging, serene core.

- I am the calm amidst the storm, recognizing that emotions are but passing clouds in my vast sky.

- I am attuned to the deeper truths, seeing beyond momentary emotional reactions to the heart of each experience.

- I am the wise sage within, understanding the impermanent nature of every feeling.

- I am resilient, transforming emotional challenges into stepping stones of growth.

- I am the silent witness, observing without judgment, understanding without entanglement.

- I am in touch with the eternal ebb and flow, embracing the highs and lows of my emotional journey.

- I am a beacon of stability, letting go of attachments to specific outcomes or emotional states.

- I am fortified by inner wisdom, drawing strength from understanding the fleeting nature of emotions.

- I am centered, not swayed by the winds of emotional turmoil, but grounded in my true self.

- I am the master alchemist, transmuting every emotion into a lesson, every experience into wisdom.

- I am the serene riverbank, watching the waters of emotion rush by, ever-present and unchanging.

- I am the embodiment of equanimity, understanding that every emotion has its purpose in the grand play of life.

- I am a vessel of peace, allowing feelings to flow through me without losing my center.

- I am the guardian of my inner sanctum, choosing which emotions to act upon and which to let go.

- I am connected to the cosmic rhythm, realizing that emotions are but ripples in the vast ocean of existence.

- I am the enlightened navigator, charting my course through the waters of emotion with grace and foresight.

- I am a beacon of clarity, shining light on the transient nature of every feeling, every moment.

- I am the harmonious balance, neither suppressing nor indulging, but simply observing the dance of emotions.

- I am rooted in the wisdom of ages, drawing upon timeless insights to navigate my emotional landscape.

- I am the master of my destiny, using emotions as tools, not letting them use me.

- I am the alchemical blend of intuition and reason, processing emotions with depth and clarity.

- I am the bridge between the ephemeral and the eternal, seeing emotions as fleeting shadows on life's canvas.

- I am the resilient oak, standing tall amidst the whirlwinds of fluctuating feelings.

- I am the mirror reflecting reality, undistorted by the hues of transient emotions.

- I am the harmonious chord resonating with universal truths, undeterred by the cacophony of temporary emotional states.

- I am the cosmic dance, embracing the full spectrum of emotions without losing my essence.

- I am the eternal flame, burning steadily, unaffected by the gusts of emotional winds.

- I am the wise alchemist, transforming even the most challenging emotions into gold.

- I am the anchor in the storm, a symbol of stability amidst the tides of emotional change.

- I am the timeless witness, experiencing every emotion, yet eternally unaltered.

- I am the sage within, calmly discerning the lessons each emotion offers.

- I am the vast sky, allowing clouds of emotion to pass, knowing they do not define my vastness.

- I am the philosopher's stone, transmuting fleeting emotions into profound wisdom.

- I am the stoic guardian, understanding the impermanence of every emotional wave.

- I am the cosmic listener, hearing the melodies of emotions without becoming their captive.

- I am the intricate pattern, where each emotion threads its color, contributing to my grand design.

- I am the silent observer, watching the theater of emotions with detached amusement.

- I am the lighthouse, guiding my soul through the foggy shores of emotional confusion.

- I am the river's source, channeling emotions with purpose and direction.

- I am the infinite horizon, where emotions rise and set, while I remain boundless and free.

A World of Connections

In the vast web of existence, every thread is intertwined, each one significant to the grand design. To fathom the mysteries of this interconnected dance is to touch the alchemical heart of our human experience. From the secluded chambers of self-reflection, the journey into the realm of social relations might seem daunting, yet it is here, amidst these interactions, that we unearth the golden nuggets of personal growth and collective evolution.

Marcus Aurelius, the stoic philosopher-emperor, once mused,

"We are made for cooperation, like feet, like hands, like eyelids, like the rows of the upper and lower teeth."

Indeed, to deny our intrinsic nature of social connection would be to overlook the alchemical principle that unity and diversity coexist. Our individual authenticity, that unique essence we each possess, isn't stifled amidst these connections. Instead, it becomes the philosopher's stone that transmutes mundane interactions into profound relationships.

Yet, in this dance of duality, it's essential to recognize that not every step will be in harmony. People, like ourselves, are learners on this grand stage of life, each moving to their rhythm, each evolving in their time. With a compassionate heart, we can embrace them, understanding that their journey is as sacred and intricate as our own.

This chapter beckons you to navigate the delicate balances of social relations, not as a chameleon who loses itself amidst myriad colors, but as the alchemist who sees the potential gold within every interaction. It is a call to nurture relationships that honor both individual authenticity and collective unity. Dive deep, dear reader, for in this alchemical process lies the key to transforming the lead of social misunderstandings into the gold of genuine connection and mutual respect.

Let's traverse the affirmations in the chapter, A World of Connections.

- I am the master of my own actions, shaping every interaction with purpose and authenticity.

- I am the alchemist of my social world, transforming every encounter into an opportunity for mutual growth.

- I am connected to all, understanding that every individual plays a unique role in the grand symphony of life.

- I am present in each moment, valuing the wisdom that every person brings into my journey.

- I am the keeper of my authenticity, never compromising my essence in the dance of social relations.

- I am attuned to the ebb and flow of interactions, knowing when to lead and when to listen.

- I am the embodiment of compassion, recognizing the divine spark within every soul I meet.

- I am resilient, navigating the complexities of relationships with grace and understanding.

- I am a beacon of unity, harmonizing differences to forge bonds of mutual respect.

- I am a seeker of depth, always striving for meaningful connections that enrich the soul.

- I am anchored in my values, ensuring that every interaction aligns with my true self.

- I am the silent observer, appreciating the lessons others teach me, even in moments of discord.

- I am a bridge builder, uniting disparate souls with the strength of my compassion and understanding.

- I am a beacon of empathy, feeling the emotions of others and offering solace and support.

- I am the catalyst of harmony, promoting peace and understanding in every social circle.

- I am secure in my solitude, recognizing that alone time enhances the quality of my social engagements.

- I am the embodiment of love, extending warmth and kindness unconditionally to all I meet.

- I am grounded, never allowing the winds of social pressures to sway my inner compass.

- I am a seeker of truth, cherishing authentic interactions over superficial exchanges.

- I am the torchbearer of trust, fostering reliability and faithfulness in my relationships.

- I am unfazed by fleeting judgments, staying true to my essence in all interactions.

- I am the master of my reactions, choosing patience and understanding over impulsivity.

- I am a source of inspiration, lifting others up with my encouragement and belief in their potential.

- I am attentive, listening more than I speak, understanding the soul behind the words.

- I am a wellspring of forgiveness, releasing grudges and embracing the growth they bring.

- I am consistent in my actions, ensuring that my words align with my deeds in all relationships.

- I am an island of calm, bringing stability and assurance to those amidst the storms of life.

- I am a guardian of boundaries, respecting my limits and those of others.

- I am an emblem of loyalty, treasuring the bond of trust shared with friends and loved ones.

- I am open-hearted, welcoming new connections while cherishing the old.

- I am the bridge that fosters connection while maintaining my own integrity and boundaries.

- In the dance of relationships, I am both a gracious leader and a respectful follower.

- I am a beacon of authenticity, attracting those who value genuine connections.

- I am mindful in my interactions, ensuring mutual respect and understanding.

- In the realm of relationships, I am steadfast in preserving my individuality and values.

- I am the gardener, nurturing the bonds that respect my boundaries and encourage mutual growth.

- While I seek harmony in connections, I am unwavering when my personal space is trespassed.

- I am the lighthouse in the sea of social interactions, guiding others with my authenticity and guarding my essence.

- In the web of relationships, I am the thread that holds its own, intertwining without losing its essence.

- I am the gatekeeper of my social realm, allowing entry to those who resonate with respect and mutual appreciation.

- I am the master of my own boundaries, understanding the sacred balance between self-respect and connection with others.

- My authenticity is unwavering; it is the beacon that draws genuine relationships towards me.

- While the world may be vast and varied, I am grounded in my own truth, never swayed by the whims of the crowd.

- In the theater of life, I play my role with sincerity, expecting nothing in return but the authenticity of others.

- Each interaction is a lesson, a mirror reflecting back a part of myself; I cherish the learnings they bring.

- I do not allow the shadows of others to dim my light; I shine brighter, illuminating the path for genuine connections.

- The judgments of others are but fleeting clouds; my self-worth remains the unyielding sky.

- I extend my hand in friendship, not out of need, but from the overflowing abundance of my spirit.

- I navigate the waters of social relations with the wisdom of sages, seeing beyond facades and understanding the essence.

- My respect for myself sets the tone for how others treat me; in my realm, I demand and give nothing short of genuine regard.

Golden Transitions

In the dance of existence, where alchemical principles intertwine with life's ever-evolving rhythm, change emerges as the eternal maestro. As understood by alchemists, transformation is not just about transmuting elements but about embracing the ebbs and flows of life's ever-changing river.

Central to this dance is the profound concept of the Void, beautifully elucidated by Alan Watts. The Void is not an abyss of nothingness but a sanctuary of infinite potential. It represents the space between what was and what will be, the silent pause between notes that gives music its melody. In this realm of Nothingness, every change, every transition, holds a promise — a promise of a new form, a new experience, a new act in the grand play of existence.

But here's the profound realization: change itself emanates from this Void. It's the very force that propels the universe forward, birthing stars, scripting stories, and creating destinies. When we grasp the concept of the Void, we begin to see change not as a force that disrupts but as a dance of the universe, choreographed in the heart of Nothingness. It's a dance that invites us to move, to grow, to shed our old selves, and to embrace the new with grace and wonder.

In this alchemical understanding, change is not a mere alteration of form but a manifestation of the Void's endless possibilities. And as we embrace this understanding, we don't just accept life's fluidity; we revel in it. We see the beauty in every transition, the magic in every moment, and the promise in every possibility.

This chapter beckons you to delve deeper into this cosmic dance. To grasp the golden threads of change and the Void, weaving them together to create a symphony that celebrates the impermanent, ever-evolving nature of life. It's an invitation to not just navigate change but to dance with it, in harmony with the universe's timeless rhythm.

Let's delve into the affirmations from the chapter, Golden Transitions.

- I am an ever-evolving dance in the vast theater of the universe.
- I am the alchemical fusion of change and stillness, finding beauty in the ebb and flow.
- I am rooted in the present, yet open to the infinite possibilities of the Void.
- I am the silence between the notes, giving melody to life's transitions.
- I am in harmony with the impermanent, embracing the endless dance of creation and dissolution.
- I am the vessel of transformation, seeing the golden potential in every moment.
- I am at peace with life's fluidity, understanding that change is the universe's loving gesture.
- I am a testament to the universe's play, where every shift carries profound meaning.
- I am attuned to the whispers of the cosmos, trusting the wisdom of its rhythm.
- I am a seeker, delving into the mysteries of the Void and the wonders it unfolds.
- I am a ripple in the vast ocean of existence, fluid and ever-changing.
- I am aligned with life's currents, drawing wisdom from its unpredictable tides.
- I am the calm embrace of the Void, finding serenity in its profound nothingness.
- I am the alchemical gold birthed from the crucible of change and impermanence.

- I am a wanderer in the cosmic play, where beginnings and endings dance in perpetual harmony.

- I am centered amidst the whirlwinds of change, knowing each gust carves a deeper truth within.

- I am a reflection of life's fleeting moments, cherishing the ephemeral beauty they bestow.

- I am tethered to the eternal, even as I navigate the shifting sands of the temporal.

- I am the silent observer, witnessing the universe weave tales of transformation and rebirth.

- I am steeped in the mysteries of the now, understanding that in the Void lies boundless potential.

- I am the ever-present witness to life's evolving narrative, grounded in its unfolding chapters.

- I am the alchemical union of past experiences and future possibilities, dancing in the present moment.

- I am attuned to the rhythm of change, celebrating each beat as a mark of growth.

- I am the quiet space between breaths, where the Void whispers its timeless wisdom.

- I am both the river and the observer, understanding that all waters eventually reach the ocean.

- I am the embrace of impermanence, seeing in it the brushstrokes of the cosmos.

- I am the alight upon the pendulum's swing, finding balance in both its rise and fall.

- I am the canvas and the artist, continuously repainting my narrative with the hues of change.

- I am the philosopher of my journey, drawing lessons from the Void's silent teachings.

- I am intertwined with the infinite dance of creation and dissolution, relishing in its cyclical grace.

- I am a beacon of adaptability, fluidly moving through life's myriad transformations.

- I am anchored in the wisdom of ages, drawing strength from the ebb and flow of existence.

- I am the dance of shadow and light, embracing the duality of the ever-changing cosmos.

- I am a testament to endurance, facing each shift with grace and resilience.

- I am an alchemical vessel, transmuting every experience into golden wisdom.

- I am attuned to the silent symphony of the universe, where every change is a note in its grand composition.

- I am a traveler through the vast expanse of time, treasuring each fleeting moment.

- I am in harmonious synchronicity with the world's pulse, intuitively navigating its seasons of change.

- I am a seeker, finding solace in the mysteries that the Void generously unfolds.

- I am the bridge between beginnings and endings, cherishing the journey that lies in between.

- I am the calm within the storm, finding serenity amidst life's inevitable upheavals.

- I am rooted in the knowledge that every ending births a new beginning.

- I am in communion with the universe, appreciating the cyclical nature of existence.

- I am a vessel of acceptance, surrendering to the rhythms of change.

- I am in sync with life's impermanent fabric, weaving my own narrative amidst its transient threads.

- I am an embodiment of metamorphosis, continuously evolving and reinventing myself.

- I am deeply connected to the infinite dance of creation and dissolution.

- I am a sentinel of time, honoring the fleeting moments that sculpt my journey.

- I am a custodian of memories, cherishing the past while gracefully sailing into the future.

- I am a reflection of the universe's grand design, gracefully adapting to the ever-shifting tides of existence.

Beyond the Stars

In the vast expanse of the cosmos, amongst billions of stars and countless galaxies, lies a curious blue dot — Earth. On this speck of cosmic dust, the human spirit, for eons, has gazed upwards, driven by an insatiable thirst to understand its place in the grand symphony of existence. Such contemplation transcends mere curiosity; it is the profound, alchemical merging of the soul's longing with the intellectual pursuit of knowledge.

Carl Sagan, the visionary cosmologist, poetically described Earth as a "pale blue dot", emphasizing our seemingly insignificant, yet uniquely special place in the universe. This perspective, rather than belittling, elevates the human experience. For in the realm of alchemy, the microcosm reflects the macrocosm. The universe outside mirrors the universe within.

Within the immeasurable expanses of the cosmos, among a sea of stars and galaxies beyond count, our world, Earth, is but a fleeting whisper. Yet, on this minor stage of the universe, the human spirit has, since time immemorial, looked upwards with a profound yearning, trying to fathom its position amidst the grand spectacle that is existence. This isn't just mere pondering; it's the soul's deep quest intertwined with an unyielding desire for understanding.

In this spiritual odyssey, much like the transformative alchemical process, we aim to transform the mundane into the enlightened, to find clarity in the ambiguous. Moving beyond established beliefs, we endeavor to explore profound questions that have lingered since the dawn of consciousness: Why do we exist? What significance do we hold? Is there a grander force, a design woven amidst the cosmic fabric?

The vastness of the cosmos is not merely an external spectacle to marvel at; it is intricately woven into the very fabric of our being.

Carl Sagan astutely observed,

> "The cosmos is within us. We are made of star-stuff. We are a way for the universe to know itself."

This profound realization ignites a deeper understanding, suggesting that our existence is not a mere accident in the grand expanse of space and time but an intrinsic part of the universe's journey of self-discovery.

Jung resonates with this cosmic dance when he declared,

> "Man is the mirror which God holds up to himself, or the sense organ with which he apprehends his being."

Thus, our search for spirituality and purpose is as much an inward exploration as it is an outward one. The same stars that glimmer in the vast, dark curtain of the sky are echoed within the depths of our souls, hinting at a profound connection, a shared destiny.

Like alchemists, with their mysterious and transformative processes, our journey in this chapter is to transmute the intangible into the known, to find clarity amid the mysteries that surround and inhabit us. We embark on this odyssey, seeking not just answers, but a deeper kinship with the cosmos and our place within it. Through this exploration, may we unravel the threads of meaning and purpose that bind us to the universe, and in doing so, come to a richer understanding of our own luminous essence.

Let's traverse the affirmations in the chapter, Beyond the Stars.

- I am a reflection of the cosmos, intricately woven into the fabric of existence.

- I am the universe experiencing itself, finding purpose in every moment.

- I am grounded in the wisdom of the ancients, guided by the stars and the inner light of consciousness.

- I am connected to the eternal Logos, finding meaning in the rhythm of the cosmos.

- I am a beacon of star-stuff, illuminating the path of spiritual discovery.

- I am the alchemical blend of matter and spirit, transforming challenges into enlightenment.

- I am in harmonious alignment with the Hermetic principles, recognizing the interconnectedness of all things.

- I am a seeker of the soul's depths, embracing both shadow and light in the journey of self-realization.

- I am attuned to the universal dance, moving gracefully with the ebb and flow of life's mysteries.

- I am the mirror reflecting the infinite, recognizing the divine spark within and all around me.

- I am in sync with the vastness of the cosmos, feeling its heartbeat within my soul.

- I am rooted in the knowledge that the universe's secrets are waiting to be uncovered within me.

- I am a channel of universal energy, transforming and transmuting experiences for higher learning.

- I am in tune with the whispers of ancient wisdom, guided by the patterns written in the stars.

- I am the embodiment of spiritual exploration, forever curious about the deeper mysteries of existence.

- I am a vessel of alchemical change, turning the base experiences of life into spiritual gold.

- I am aligned with the Stoic Logos, seeing reason and purpose in every event of life.

- I am connected to the age-old teachings of Hermeticism, understanding as above, so below; as within, so without.

- I am a beacon of cosmic consciousness, drawing insights from the vast expanse of the universe.

- I am on a quest of inner discovery, heeding the call of the soul to find true purpose.

- I am an intricate part of the universe's grand design, with every thought and action having its purpose.

- I am receptive to the synchronicities that Carl Jung speaks of, recognizing the meaningful coincidences in my life.

- I am bound by the timeless wisdom of the ancients, drawing strength from their teachings and experiences.

- I am a testament to the interconnectedness of all, understanding that everything is a reflection of the whole.

- I am the alchemist of my own soul, continuously refining my spirit in the crucible of life.

- I am in alignment with the Stoic principle of amor fati, loving and accepting everything that life presents to me.

- I am in harmony with the cosmic dance, celebrating the rhythms and cycles of existence.

- I am an explorer of the inner realms, seeking the treasures of self-awareness and enlightenment.

- I am the bridge between the seen and the unseen, understanding the dual nature of reality.

- I am constantly evolving, guided by the ever-expanding consciousness of the universe.

- I am a manifestation of the cosmos, living out its story through my unique journey.

- I am deeply attuned to the mysteries that lie beyond the veil, seeking knowledge and wisdom from both seen and unseen sources.

- I am a beacon of light, shining my essence amidst the vastness of the universe, echoing Carl Jung's belief that the individual illuminates the collective.

- I am grounded in the present while maintaining a cosmic perspective, understanding the transient nature of earthly experiences.

- I am unyielding in my pursuit of inner truth, embracing the Stoic notion that the logos — the universal reason — is within me.

- I am an eternal student of the universe, drawing insights from the vast reservoir of collective knowledge.

- I am the convergence of spirit and matter, a testament to alchemical processes shaping both the macrocosm and microcosm.

- I am one with the Hermetic principle "As above, so below," recognizing the harmonious relationship between the inner and outer worlds.

- I am the embodiment of star-stuff, as Carl Sagan professed, ever-reminded of my cosmic origin.

- I am in perpetual dialogue with the universe, understanding that every moment is an opportunity for deeper communion and insight.

- I am an instrument of the universe, here to understand and reflect its vast wisdom.

- I am undeterred by the ephemeral, grounding myself in the eternal truths of existence.

- I am intricately woven into the fabric of life, with each thread representing a lesson, an experience, or a revelation.

- I am a guardian of my inner world, safeguarding its sanctity against the noise of external distractions.

- I am the synthesis of past, present, and future, drawing strength from the Stoic belief that all is connected by the logos.

- I am a seeker on the alchemical path, constantly refining and purifying my essence in the crucible of life's experiences.

- I am a reflection of the cosmos, embodying Carl Jung's vision of humanity as the mirror through which the universe sees itself.

- I am boundless in my exploration of the self, recognizing that my depths echo the vastness of the universe.

- I am aligned with the Hermetic wisdom that the mind molds reality, understanding my thoughts and intentions shape my destiny.

- I am a bridge between the earthly and the celestial, embracing my dual nature as both a being of matter and spirit.

In Mastery of the Self

Whoa, hold up! Before you close this book and go about making coffee or whatever, let's take a moment. From the get-go, we didn't just flip pages here—we went full Indiana Jones into the catacombs of our souls, didn't we? It's been a wild ride, a treasure hunt where X marks the spot right where you're sitting.

Transforming base metals into gold? Cool, but we've been busy turning our everyday blahs into Aha! moments. It's like alchemy, but with more existential oomph. We've squared up to our fears, done the mental gymnastics, surfed the big waves of our feelings —and hey, we didn't drown!

Choices, choices everywhere. We've learned it's not just about picking pizza toppings. Real choice is about mastering the chaos inside so you can chill in the eye of the storm. Freedom isn't just about doing what you want—it's about not being a puppet to past pains or future freak-outs.

Then there's the whole people thing. We've untangled some of those knotty relationships and figured out that setting boundaries isn't about building walls; it's more like drawing a map that shows where my funky little world ends and yours begins. And guess what? Every soul we meet is holding up a mirror, showing us bits of ourselves—pretty, gritty, all of it.

Change—yeah, that beast. We've learned to give it a bear hug. Nothing sticks around forever, and that's not a doom-scroll; it's a scroll of freedom. Everything morphs, everything flows. And through this ever-spinning cosmic kaleidoscope, we remember: nothing really ends; it just shape-shifts.

Oh, and we shot for the stars, literally wandered cosmic realms, channeling our inner Carl Sagan because, why not? We're stardust on a cosmic quest, after all.

But hey, the plot twist? The journey doesn't end when you hit the back cover. Nope, it's just a pit stop. What we've learned and loved and wondered at—that's the gold. The real magic trick is to keep the show going, to keep evolving, questing, connecting with the grand everything.

Now, lean in for the secret sauce—the mystical key. Before you can dance with Kali in the wild abandon of cosmic destruction and creation, you gotta find your inner Shiva, the chill lord of the cosmic dance himself. It's about balancing that fierce energy with some cool cosmic poise. They're like cosmic partners in the dance of our own search for the absolute, the beyond, the transcendent—whatever that may be for you.

So here we are, at the not-end of our tale. In the words of those old-timey wisdom rockstars, the Stoics, and the mystical alchemists: This isn't "The End." Oh no, it's just another groovy beginning. Because mastering this wild ride of being you? That's the real destination. And you're exactly where you need to be—here, now, perfectly placed in the messy, beautiful now.

So, here's the skinny: as we shimmy off the last page and pirouette into the great unknown, remember that every step, stumble, and groove in this boogie called life has its rhythm. Don't sweat the missteps or the slow jams; they're just part of your playlist. There's no rush, no finish line where someone's handing out medals for 'Most Enlightened' or 'Best Spiritual Journey.' It's all about the dance, the movement from one moment to the next, savoring the swing and sway of the now.

And when you find yourself fretting over the ifs and buts, just pause, take a breath, and listen. Because in that breath, in that heartbeat of stillness, you'll find clarity—a moment of peace where everything seems to say, 'Hey, you're exactly where you're meant to be.'

Embrace the spiral of life, with all its chaos and cosmos, knowing that each turn brings a new perspective, a new spark. From the alchemical fires of transformation to the serene orbits of celestial contemplation, keep dancing, keep dreaming, keep diving deep.

And in the spirit of our journey, as we scatter to the four winds, let's not say goodbye. Instead, let's promise to meet in that mystic meadow, the one Rumi talked about. Because, as the Sufi poet Rumi once wrote,

"Out beyond ideas of wrongdoing and right-doing, there is a field. I'll meet you there."

Printed in Great Britain
by Amazon